Managing the Incompetent Teacher

Second Edition

Managing the Incompetent Teacher

Edwin M. Bridges
with the assistance of
Barry Groves

CLEARINGHOUSE ON EDUCATIONAL MANAGEMENT
COLLEGE OF EDUCATION · UNIVERSITY OF OREGON

Design: University Publications, University of Oregon

International Standard Book Number: 0-86552-102-6
Library of Congress Catalog Card Number: 90-80371
ERIC/CEM School Management Digest Series, Number 33
ERIC/CEM Accession Number: EA 021 575

Printed in the United States of America, 1990
ERIC Clearinghouse on Educational Management
University of Oregon, Eugene OR 97403

Copyright © 1990 University of Oregon, 1787 Agate Street,
Eugene, OR 97403. All rights reserved.

Prior to publication, this manuscript was submitted for critical review and determination of professional competence. The publication has met such standards. The publication was prepared with funding from the Office of Educational Research and Improvement, U.S. Department of Education under contract no. OERI-R 188062004. The opinions expressed in this report do not necessarily reflect the positions or policies of the Department of Education. No federal funds were used in the printing of this publication.

The University of Oregon is an equal opportunity, affirmative action institution committed to cultural diversity.

Mission of ERIC and the Clearinghouse

The Educational Resources Information Center (ERIC) is a national information system operated by the U.S. Department of Education. ERIC serves the educational community by disseminating research results and other resource information that can be used in developing more effective educational programs.

The ERIC Clearinghouse on Educational Management, one of several such units in the system, was established at the University of Oregon in 1966. The Clearinghouse and its companion units process research reports and journal articles for announcement in ERIC's index and abstract bulletins.

Research reports are announced in *Resources in Education (RIE)*, available in many libraries and by subscription from the United States Government Printing Office, Washington, D.C. 20402.

Most of the documents listed in *RIE* can be purchased through the ERIC Document Reproduction Service, operated by Computer Microfilm International Corporation.

Journal articles are announced in *Current Index to Journals in Education*. *CIJE* is also available in many libraries and can be ordered from Oryx Press, 2214 North Central at Encanto, Phoenix, Arizona 85004. Semiannual cumulations can be ordered separately.

Besides processing documents and journal articles, the Clearinghouse prepares bibliographies, literature reviews, monographs, and other interpretive research studies on topics in its educational area.

Clearinghouse National Advisory Board

Jim Bencivenga, Education Editor, The Christian Science Monitor

Gordon Cawelti, Executive Director, Association for Supervision and Curriculum Development

Timothy J. Dyer, Executive Director, National Association of Secondary School Principals

Patrick Forsyth, Executive Director, University Council for Educational Administration

Joyce G. McCray, Executive Director, Council for American Private Education

Richard D. Miller, Executive Director, American Association of School Administrators

Samuel Sava, Executive Director, National Association of Elementary School Principals

Thomas Shannon, Executive Director, National School Boards Association

Don I. Tharpe, Executive Director, Association of School Business Officials International

Gene Wilhoit, Executive Director, National Association of State Boards of Education

ADMINISTRATIVE STAFF
Philip K. Piele, Professor and Director
Keith A. Acheson, Associate Director
Stuart C. Smith, Director of Publications

The authors wish to thank James G. Seely and Henry M. Levin for their valuable comments on an earlier draft of this paper.

Preface

The first edition of *Managing the Incompetent Teacher*, published in 1984, was to become during the next five years the best-selling monograph of the ERIC Clearinghouse on Educational Management. Thousands of school district officials across the nation have come to rely on this book for implementing policies and procedures that ensure a high quality of teaching in their districts.

Because of the book's high degree of acceptance, we are pleased to offer this timely revision, which adds significant new information in such areas as criteria for evaluating a teacher's effectiveness, use of student test scores for teacher evaluation, peer evaluation, evaluation of teachers by parents, remediation procedures, and grounds for dismissal. In addition, the final chapter, Putting Theory into Practice, has been rewritten in its entirety.

We acknowledge the role of the Institute for Research on Educational Finance and Governance (IFG) at Stanford University, which funded the preparation of the first edition.

The author, Edwin M. Bridges, is a professor of education in the Administration and Policy Analysis program at Stanford University. Barry Groves is Director of Personnel, Lucia Mar Unified School District, California. Formerly Dr. Bridges served as director of the Midwest Administration Center at the University of Chicago. His current research focuses on the practices used by school administrators in dealing with the problem of incompetent teachers. Dr. Bridges has also written extensively on problems of handling teacher absenteeism and shared decision-making. His treatment of these problems appears in such journals as *The Administrative Science Quarterly, Educational Administration Quarterly,* and *Administrator's Notebook*.

Philip K. Piele
Director, ERIC/CEM

Contents

Introduction   1
    Tenure   2
    Incompetence   3
    Dismissal   5
    Dismissal of Tenured Teachers for Incompetence   6
    An Organizational Approach to the Dismissal of Incompetent Teachers   8

Establish "Excellence in Teaching" as a District Priority   9
    Symbolic Leadership   9
    Existing Organizational Routines   10
    New Organizational Routines   11
    Interdistrict Cooperation   12

Adopt and Publish Criteria for Evaluating Teachers   13
    Legal Considerations   13
    Professional Considerations   15
    Scientific Considerations   16
    Practical Considerations   16

Determine Whether Teachers Satisfy the Criteria   19
    Supervisor Ratings   19
    Student Ratings   22
    Student Test Results   23
    Peer Evaluations   26
    Self-Evaluations   27
    Parent Evaluations   29
    Student and Parent Complaints   30
    Implications   31

Provide Appropriate Remediation   33
    Causes of Poor Performance   34
    Types of Remediation   35

Length of Remediation   38

Ensure That Supervisors Have the Requisite Competencies   41
   Competencies   41
   Competency Assurance Programs   51

Provide the Necessary Resources   53
   Time   53
   Authority   54
   Access to Remedial Assistance   55
   Access to Legal Counsel   56
   Support   57

Hold Supervisors Accountable   58
   Inflated Ratings   58
   Procrastination and Rationalization   59
   Buck-Passing   60
   Instructional Leadership   61

Provide Fair Hearing Prior to Dismissal   63
   Components of a Fair Hearing   63
   Phases of Dismissal Proceedings   64

Putting Theory into Practice   69
   Situational Appraisal   69
   Legitimization   70
   Teacher Involvement   70
   Full Accounting   71
   Continual Commitment   71

Appendix: District Evaluation Practices Inventory (DEPI)   73

Bibliography   77

Managing the Incompetent Teacher

Introduction

Incompetence in the teaching profession is a problem of major importance to publicly supported elementary and secondary schools. Since 1969, the Gallup organization has conducted an annual poll of the public's attitudes toward the public schools. The results of these surveys, reported in the September issues of the *Phi Delta Kappan*, are painfully consistent. Public school parents express serious concerns about the quality of teaching in their local schools. For twenty consecutive years, public school parents have identified this particular problem as one of the biggest problems facing the schools in their community. Teaching quality is mentioned as the biggest problem with the fourth or fifth greatest frequency; only once does it drop as low as seventh. On one occasion 45 percent of the public school parents indicated that there were teachers in the local schools who should be fired. The most frequently cited reason for this drastic action was incompetence; it equalled all other reasons combined.

The quality of the teaching force is of even greater concern to school administrators. In three polls conducted by the American Association of School Administrators in 1974, 1976, and 1977, superintendents rated "incompetent staff" as one of their top three administrative problems (Neill and Custis 1978). More recently, California principals indicated in a statewide survey that 11 percent of their teachers were unsatisfactory performers in the classroom (Groves 1985).

In response to the perceived prevalence and seriousness of incompetent performance in the classroom, numerous solutions have been advanced such as: (1) cleanse the profession by dismissing the incompetent teachers; (2) improve the attractiveness of the teaching profession by raising salaries; (3) restrict entry into the profession by means of competency tests; (4) upgrade the quality of preservice teacher education by adopting competency-based preparation programs; and (5) provide incentives for quality teaching by instituting merit pay (Citron 1985). This discussion will concentrate on the first proposed solution—dismissal of the incompetent teacher. Special emphasis will be placed on the tenured teacher who is incompetent in performing his or her classroom teaching duties.

When discussing the dismissal of tenured teachers for incompetence in the classroom, we intend to examine this issue from the vantage point of the superintendent of schools. In particular, we shall describe eight elements of an organizational approach that the chief executive officer should implement in his or her district to identify incompetent teachers and to dismiss them if they are unable to improve their performance. This approach represents a potentially effective response to three sets of interrelated problems: (1) the legal barriers to removing tenured teachers for incompetence in the classroom; (2) the technical problems in measuring teacher effectiveness; and (3) the human obstacles that are involved, including the willingness and the ability of supervisors to carry out their responsibilities for teacher evaluation, remediation, and dismissal. However, before delineating the various components of this organizational approach, we need to clarify the meaning of three crucial terms—tenure, incompetence, and dismissal.

TENURE

Tenure is an employment status conferred by state law on teachers who successfully complete a trial or probationary period usually lasting from two to five years. Once teachers have attained this employment status they have the right to continued possession of their jobs. This right constitutes a property right under the Fourteenth Amendment of the United States Constitution and may be taken away only if the employer proves that there is cause for dismissal and provides the teacher with procedural due process.

The legal causes for dismissal and the procedural due process rights of the tenured teacher are generally enumerated in the state education code. Some common causes for dismissal are incompetence, insubordination, immorality, and neglect of duty. As for the procedural due process rights, the specific details vary from one state to the other; however, the major elements remain virtually the same. A tenured teacher is entitled to a fair hearing that entails a timely and adequate notice of reasons and charges, representation by legal counsel, an opportunity to cross-examine witnesses, an impartial hearing by individuals who do not present or prosecute the case for dismissal, and a decision that is based only on evidence presented at the hearing.

The fundamental purpose behind tenure is to protect adequate and competent teachers from arbitrary and unreasonable dismissals by school boards. Prior to enactment of state tenure laws, teachers served at the pleasure of school boards. With their authority and power to dismiss unchecked, some boards engaged in a variety of questionable practices. Teachers were dismissed to make places for friends and relatives of board members, to save money by diminishing the number of teachers and increasing the workload of those retained, to lower costs by creating vacancies to be filled by inexperienced teachers, and to punish those who were "disloyal" to the administration (Lebeis 1939). Such practices stimulated state and national teacher associations to press for tenure legislation as early as 1915. By 1980 nearly every state had adopted statewide tenure (Stelzer and Banthin 1980).

Although teacher tenure has become widespread, it lacks support from the majority of school board members, school administrators, and parents. For example, in 1975, 95 percent of the school board members interviewed in Louisiana favored reform of the state's teacher tenure law (Cramer 1976). A nationwide survey of school administrators in 1972 showed that 86 percent wanted tenure reformed or abolished (Cramer). Parents with children in the public schools have consistently expressed opposition to tenure for teachers in the Gallup polls of attitudes toward public education; on four different occasions between 1970 and 1977 more than half of the parents surveyed indicated that they opposed teacher tenure (Elam 1979). Despite the prevalence of this opposition, there is little likelihood that tenure will be abolished given the political strength and treasuries of teacher associations. Job security is the number one priority of these groups, understandably so, given the past practices of some school boards and the current difficulties of professionals in locating employment appropriate to their level of training (Kaufman 1982).

INCOMPETENCE

Most state legislatures have singled out incompetence (or one of its blood relatives—inefficiency, gross inefficiency, and inadequate performance) as a legal cause for dismissing tenured teachers. Only two states have attempted to define *incompetence*, however. Alaska defines incompetency as "the inability or the unintentional or intentional failure to perform the teacher's customary teaching duties in a satisfactory manner" (Alaska Education Code, Section 14-20-170), while Tennessee defines incompetency as

> being incapable; lacking adequate power, capacity or ability to carry out the duties and responsibilities of the position. This may apply to physical, mental, educational, emotional or other personal conditions. It may include lack of training or experience. Evident unfitness for service; physical, mental or emotional condition unfitting a teacher to instruct or associate with children; or inability to command respect for subordinates or to secure cooperation of those with whom he must work. (Tennes-

see Code Annotated, 49-1401)

Both definitions encompass instructional and noninstructional duties; neither supplies any criteria for determining what constitutes incompetent performance in the classroom. To obtain insight into the legal meaning of incompetent teaching, one must turn to other sources—case law, policies of state boards of education, and statutory law relating to the evaluation of certificated personnel.

Judges also have shown little inclination to specify standards by which incompetence in the classroom can be evaluated. One notable exception, however, is the Michigan Court of Appeals, which stated in 1976 that

> School boards and the Tenure Commission should, in each case, make specific determinations concerning the challenged teacher's *knowledge of his subject, his ability to impart it, the manner and efficacy of his discipline over his students, his rapport with parents and other teachers, and his physical and mental ability to withstand the strain of teaching*. In each case, the effect on the school and its students of the acts alleged to require dismissal must be delineated. (*Beebee v. Haslett Pub. Sch.*, 66 Mich. App., 718 at 726 [1979])

The Michigan Tenure Commission subsequently adopted these criteria as its definition of incompetency but held that all five factors need not be established to support a charge of incompetence. Any one of these factors is sufficient (*Niemi v. Bd. of Educ.*, Kearsley Sch. Dist., TTC 74-36).

Some states' legislatures require their state boards of education to adopt criteria for evaluating individuals who are teaching under continuing contracts (a form of tenure). These criteria in effect constitute the legal definition of incompetence for teachers in that state. One state board of education (South Carolina), for example, has adopted the following criteria for evaluating tenured teachers: long-term planning, short-term planning, clarifying rules and procedures, disciplining inappropriate behavior, organizing instruction, clarifying the goals of instruction, teaching new content, practicing and reviewing content, maintaining student involvement in learning, and monitoring student progress. These ten criteria were selected on the basis of a review of the literature, a survey of educators in the state, and the work of a committee composed of superintendents, personnel administrators, principals, and teachers.

Insight into the legal meaning of incompetent teaching also may be obtained by examining state statutes regulating the evaluation of certificated personnel. Although state statutes rarely specify the criteria for evaluating teachers, courts may choose to interpret the meaning of incompetence in terms of these criteria when they are specified. In

Washington, for example, the dismissal law is read in combination with the statute on evaluation, which sets out the following categories: instructional skill, classroom management, professional preparation and scholarship, effort toward improvement when needed, the handling of student discipline and related problems, interest in teaching pupils, and knowledge of subject matter.

If the legal meaning of incompetence has not been clarified in any of the aforementioned ways, local boards of education have considerable leeway in defining what incompetence means in their individual districts. The development of a reasonable and appropriate definition of incompetence is the subject of a later section that centers on issues related to the adoption and publication of criteria for judging the effectiveness of teachers.

DISMISSAL

Tenure provides teachers with a protective shield against arbitrary, capricious dismissal; but it does not guarantee them a life-time job. When a local board of education believes there is sufficient cause (such as incompetence), the board may elect to dismiss the teacher. Dismissal occurs when the board of education decides to terminate the employment of the teacher and records this action in its official minutes. As a result of this decision, the teacher is involuntarily removed from the district's payroll and is denied all other benefits, rights, and privileges of employment.

Dismissal is not to be confused with a forced resignation. Although the teacher leaves the organization against his or her will in both instances, the forced resignation provides the teacher with an opportunity to save face because the organization records his departure as a voluntary exit. In anticipation of a decision to dismiss, the board or one of its designees may offer the teacher an opportunity to request early retirement or to submit a resignation. The board may also quietly agree to provide the teacher with some type of inducement (for example, cash, medical coverage, and outplacement counseling) in exchange for his resignation or early retirement (Bridges 1990). These arrangements enable the teacher to avert possible revocation of his or her teaching credential and to avoid the public humiliation and professional stigma that may accompany what some refer to as the corporate equivalent of capital punishment—dismissal. Not surprisingly, induced resignations and early retirements are much more common than dismissal (Bridges 1990), and they are the preferred mode of separation for both teachers and administrators.

DISMISSAL OF TENURED TEACHERS FOR INCOMPETENCE

Dismissal of tenured teachers for incompetence is a relatively rare occurrence. Only one teacher in the state of Florida lost a teaching certificate for reason of incompetency during the 1977-78 school year (Dolgin 1981). There were only eleven dismissal cases due to incompetence appealed to the Pennsylvania secretary of education for adjudication between March 1971 and April 1976 (Finlayson 1979). From 1977 to 1987 only twenty tenured teachers were dismissed for incompetence in the entire state of New York (Gross 1988). In Illinois only sixty-nine tenured teachers were discharged for incompetence between 1976 and 1988 (Thurston forthcoming).

When tenured teachers are dismissed for incompetence, one or more of the following types of failure are usually involved (Bridges and Gumport 1984):

1. Technical failure. The teacher's expertise falls short of what the task requires. Technical failure is indicated by deficiencies in one or more of the following: discipline, teaching methods, knowledge of subject matter, explanation of concepts, evaluation of pupil performance, organization, planning, lesson plans, and homework assignments.

2. Bureaucratic failure. The teacher fails to comply with school/district rules and regulations or directives of superiors. Bureaucratic failure is indicated by the teacher's failure to follow suggestions for improving his or her performance, to adhere to the content of the district's curriculum, or to allow supervisors in the classroom for purposes of observing the teacher's performance.

3. Ethical failure. The teacher fails to conform to standards of conduct presumably applicable to members of the teaching profession. Violations of these standards commonly take the form of physical or psychological abuse of students, negative attitudes toward students, and indifferent performance of one's teaching duties.

4. Productive failure. The teacher fails to obtain certain desirable results in the classroom. Productive failure is indicated by the academic progress of students, the interest of students in what is being taught, the attitudes of students toward school, the respect of students for the teacher, and the climate of the classroom.

5. Personal failure. The teacher lacks certain cognitive, affective, or physical attributes deemed instrumental in teaching. Indicators of personal deficiencies include poor judgment, emotional instability, lack of self-control, and insufficient strength to withstand the rigors of teaching.

These five types of failure do not occur with equal frequency in cases involving the dismissal of tenured teachers. Contrary to the situation that exists in the professions of law and medicine, the most prevalent type of failure is technical; more than 80 percent of the tenured dismissal cases involve this kind of failure (Bridges 1983). The leading indicator of technical failure is deficiency in maintaining discipline. Interestingly, weakness in discipline emerges as a leading cause for dismissal in every study of teacher failure conducted since 1913 (Littler 1914, Buellesfield 1915, Madsen 1927, Simon 1936, Bridges and Gumport 1984, Gross 1988, and Thurston forthcoming). Bureaucratic failure figures in half of the cases, followed in order of frequency by ethical failure (44 percent), productive failure (34 percent), and personal failure (17 percent) (Bridges and Gumport 1984).

In the majority of dismissal cases, there is something approaching a "performance collapse." When tenured teachers are dismissed, they often are charged with multiple sources of failure and one or more of the other legal grounds for dismissal such as neglect of duty, conduct unbecoming a teacher, and other good and just causes. Dismissal rarely stems from a single unforgivable, egregious error; rather, termination is based upon a pattern of mistakes and failure that persists over periods ranging from several months to several years (Bridges and Gumport 1984, Tigges).

Regardless of the character of the teacher's failure, the success of a school board that attempts to dismiss tenured teachers is by no means ensured. Approximately one-third of the eighty-six dismissal cases that Bridges and Gumport (1984) examined between 1939 and 1982 were overturned upon appeal. In nearly one-half of the cases examined by Thurston (forthcoming) between 1976 and 1988, the district's decision was overturned and the teacher was reinstated. However, Thurston noted a trend over the past five years for district dismissal decisions to be upheld rather than overturned.

If a dismissal decision is reversed, school officials face the need to reinstate the teacher and to cope with the aftermath of reinstatement. When terminated teachers return to their former employers, the results are generally dismal from the district's point of view. Most of the teachers who are rated poor at the time of termination are also rated poor after reinstatement (Gold and others 1978). The same difficulties that originally led to termination recur in the vast majority of cases. Moreover, reversals subsequently lead to a bad atmosphere between labor and management and additional problems at the bargaining table. These negative results are consistent with those found in studies of reinstatement in the private sector (Jones 1961, McDermott and Newhams 1971, Malinowski 1981).

AN ORGANIZATIONAL APPROACH TO THE DISMISSAL OF INCOMPETENT TEACHERS

Most teachers in our nation's schools are competent, conscientious, hardworking individuals. All too often their efforts are overshadowed by the poor performance of a relatively small number of incompetent classroom teachers. These incompetents must be identified and assisted, and if they fail to improve, dismissed. School districts that wish to confront this challenge face a formidable array of legal, technical, and human problems. These problems can be overcome, however, if school districts are willing to adopt an organizational approach to deal with incompetent teachers in an integrated, comprehensive fashion. The eight elements comprising a useful approach are as follows:

1. Establish "excellence in teaching" as a high priority for the district.
2. Adopt and publish reasonable criteria for evaluating teachers.
3. Adopt sound procedures for determining whether teachers satisfy these criteria and apply these procedures uniformly to teachers in the district.
4. Provide unsatisfactory teachers with remediation (assistance) and a reasonable period of time to improve.
5. Establish and implement procedures for ensuring that appraisers have the requisite competencies.
6. Provide appraisers with the resources needed to carry out their responsibilities.
7. Hold appraisers accountable for evaluating and dealing with incompetent teachers.
8. Provide incompetent teachers with a fair hearing prior to making the dismissal decision.

Superintendents who follow this systematic approach reap several noteworthy benefits. In districts that use this approach, principals are much more likely to confront the poor performers and to induce resignations or early retirements if they fail to improve (Groves 1985). Moreover, in those schools where principals are issuing formal notices of incompetence and inducing incompetents to leave, the students' achievement tends to be higher than in those schools where principals tend to ignore the problem of poor performance (Groves 1985, McLaughlin 1984). Finally, the administration is much more likely to have its dismissal decisions upheld if the teacher chooses to contest the decision, rather than to resign or retire early.

1

Establish "Excellence in Teaching" as a District Priority

Any organization faces a myriad of problems, opportunities, and demands that compete for the attention of organizational decision-makers. The outcome of this competition often depends on the significance attached to the various issues by the chief executive officer (CEO). If the CEO assigns a high priority to a particular issue, subordinates are more apt to place that issue high on their own agenda. If, on the other hand, the chief executive is indifferent to the issue, this indifference will be reproduced in the minds and actions of people up and down the organizational ladder. The task of the school superintendent, the district's chief executive officer, is, therefore, to ensure that "excellence in teaching" becomes and remains a centerpiece on the agenda of the district.

There are several ways in which the superintendent can heighten a district's concern for competent classroom performance; some of the possibilities include:

1. provide symbolic leadership
2. incorporate the commitment into existing organizational routines
3. establish new organizational routines where none currently exist
4. cooperate with other districts to bring about the reforms needed to maintain quality teaching performance

SYMBOLIC LEADERSHIP

As the head of the organization, the superintendent is in a unique position to provide symbolic leadership. Such leadership involves the development of a consensus within the organization about those activities that are most highly valued by the organization. The superintendent can emphasize the importance of teaching by spending time on issues related to this activity, by making public pronouncements on the importance and value of teaching, and by creating slogans and organizational processes that reflect a commitment to high quality teaching.

Dr. Paul Sakamoto, superintendent of the Mountain View-Los Altos School District (California), is a prime example of a school superintendent who has provided symbolic leadership for excellence in teaching (McLaughlin and Pfiefer 1988). His "Management Practices Plan" describes a set of administrative guidelines to develop "a unique organizational culture which believes in excellence through people and which develops a sense of family among its members." According to Sakamoto,

> Evaluation is the key to any comprehensive program of instructional improvement...the key to what goes on in schools. If high levels of student achievement are really our goal, then we should be focusing here. Teachers feel isolated, that no one cares, and just close the door. Evaluation opens the door up.

The imprint of Sakamoto's philosophy on the district is unmistakable. In the words of a department head, "Sakamoto really runs things in this district. His philosophy pervades the whole district and he sets the style."

Superior teaching performance is an important component of this philosophy as revealed in these comments by one of the district's principals:

> In this district, we see the average teacher as someone who needs improvement. Here, in Los Altos, satisfactory isn't good enough.... The Superintendent here makes it very clear that we want only the very best teachers in this district.

EXISTING ORGANIZATIONAL ROUTINES

Two important, recurring aspects of school district operation are collective bargaining and preparation of the annual budget. Both of these activities involve trade-offs among important, but conflicting objectives; consequently, these two activities provide the superintendent and the school board with an opportunity to demonstrate or to undermine their public commitment to quality teaching. In light of the intense political pressures that are likely to develop in connection with collective bargaining and budget preparation, these two activities represent critical testing and proving grounds for the administrator's commitment.

Thus far, school officials appear to have neglected their commitment to quality teaching at the bargaining table. Studies conducted in the late 1960s and early 1970s show that the supervisory roles of principals have been seriously impaired by negotiations (Educational Research Service 1979). This erosion of the principal's authority to supervise and evaluate teachers is due in part to the absence of any overriding commitment to "excellence in teaching" during the process of negotiations. Neither management nor labor seems to use any rules or principles for making trade-offs among the items being negotiated (for example, salary, class size, school calendar, teacher transfer, and teacher evaluation); rather, both sides act on a case-by-case basis (McDonnell and Pascal 1979). If school officials are to recover their lost prerogatives or to preserve existing ones, they must in the future exhibit greater concern for the role of trade-offs in negotiations and adopt priorities for the negotiations process that reflect the district's commitment to competent classroom teaching. Otherwise, trade-offs are likely to be made on the basis of personal self-interests or political expedience.

Preparation of the budget is not independent of collective bargaining and is, therefore, subject to the same sort of intense political pressures. Educational institutions are labor-intensive; consequently, salaries may account for up to 85 percent of a school district's budget. Teacher unions are generally interested in increasing this percentage and in distributing the salary gains on the basis of seniority and level of educational training rather than merit as is the prevailing practice for professionals employed in the private sector (Peck 1981). Collective bargaining is the primary process used by teachers to attain their salary objectives.

The economic interests of teacher unions may collide with important programmatic concerns of school officials. If teachers demand higher salaries at the bargaining table and school officials meet these wage demands, there will be less money available for other programs, including those related to teacher evaluation and dismissal (for example, inservice education for principals and merit pay for exceptional performance by supervisors). To maintain the fiscal integrity of such programs, the superintendent and school board must set firm targets prior to negotiations. The importance of funding level targets should not be underestimated, as level of aspiration at the outset of negotiations is a major determinant of success at the bargaining table.

NEW ORGANIZATIONAL ROUTINES

Providing symbolic leadership and using existing activities like collective bargaining and preparation of the annual budget are important ways in which superintendents can demonstrate their commitment to teaching excellence, but they are not the only means. Superintendents may also scrutinize the approach used by their district in evaluating and dismissing incompetent teachers. This organizational examination may proceed by completing the District Evaluation Practices Inventory (DEPI) contained in the Appendix. If the review reveals that one or more of the features of the organizational approach that we recommend have been omitted, the superintendent can attempt to locate the obstacles that block implementation and endeavor to remove them before proceeding to install these new organizational procedures. The initiation of these additional elements in the organization's approach to evaluation and dismissal will heighten the significance attached to competent teaching performance by principals and teachers alike.

INTERDISTRICT COOPERATION

A final way in which superintendents can act as idea-champions for "excellence in teaching" is by promoting cooperation with other school districts. Some of the obstacles or constraints facing local districts cannot be eliminated by working solely within the boundaries of the organization. State statutes, for example, often prescribe the causes for dismissal, the procedures to be followed, and the legal entitlements of teachers prior to and following dismissal. These state-imposed impediments are unlikely to be changed unless local boards of education and superintendents orchestrate their efforts across districts in support of such reform.

Funding arrangements provide another example of the possibilities for interdistrict cooperation. While teacher groups lobby at the state level to increase the funds potentially available for salaries, school officials should spearhead efforts to obtain categorical aid for staff development and evaluation. If these efforts are unsuccessful, local districts should pool their limited resources and establish joint programs such as in-service training for evaluators and remediation of unsatisfactory teachers.

Each of the aforementioned ways in which superintendents can underscore their commitment to competent performance in the classroom may be used alone or in combination with one or more of the other possibilities. The paths that a superintendent actually chooses to follow will depend to some extent on his or her perceptions of the needs and conditions existing in the district. If his predecessor has emphasized "excellence in teaching," implemented all the elements of an organizational approach to evaluation and dismissal, and secured the necessary funding, the superintendent simply needs to affirm his intention to continue the commitment and to preserve the integrity of the approach when the budget is prepared and a contract is negotiated with the teachers. If, on the other hand, the superintendent faces the need to recover lost ground, he may need to exert symbolic leadership in a forceful manner and to enlist the full support of the board of education before utilizing *all* the other ways that we have suggested.

Adopt and Publish Criteria for Evaluating Teachers

Criteria play an important role in the evaluation and dismissal of a tenured teacher for incompetence. They designate those factors on which the quality of the teacher's performance will be assessed. A major function of these criteria is to provide teachers with advance notice about the meaning of competent performance so that they will know where to direct their efforts and skills. If a school district has not adopted and published such criteria, courts are likely to overturn a district's dismissal decision on the grounds that the tenured teacher has been denied a basic aspect of due process guaranteed by the Fourteenth Amendment.

Unfortunately, many districts are not meeting their legal obligations to adopt and/or to publish the criteria they use in judging the effectiveness of their teachers. Teachers report that they do not know what criteria are being used by their principals to evaluate the performance of teachers. Moreover, they complain that the criteria vary from one school to another within the same district (Natriello and Dornbusch 1980-81).

To prevent these circumstances from arising, the superintendent needs to take at least three actions if the board has adopted criteria for evaluating its teachers: (l) provide teachers with a copy of these criteria; (2) require principals to review these criteria with teachers at the beginning of each school year; and (3) hold principals accountable for applying these criteria uniformly throughout the district.

If the board has not adopted any criteria, the superintendent should first recommend criteria that take into account several types of considerations—legal, professional, scientific, and practical.

LEGAL CONSIDERATIONS

In choosing the criteria to be used in evaluating the competence of classroom teachers, superintendents and local boards of education generally have considerable leeway. Courts realize that the evaluation of teachers (like the evaluation of lawyers) is a highly subjective undertaking and that there is no consensus within the teaching profession as to what constitutes adequate or competent performance. In the absence of state legislation to the contrary, courts are inclined to accept without question the criteria employed by local school districts in evaluating classroom teachers, as long as these criteria are job-related (Beckham 1985). Criteria that have appeared in previous dismissal cases heard at the appellate court level are as follows:

1. knowledge of the subject matter
2. ability to impart knowledge effectively
3. ability to obtain the respect of parents and students
4. proper use of corporal punishment
5. willingness to accept teaching advice from superiors
6. adequate academic progress of students
7. ability to maintain discipline
8. physical ability to perform the duties of a teacher
9. emotional stability (Tigges)

Although persistent failure to satisfy any one of these criteria is sufficient grounds for dismissal, most court cases involve more than one criterion.

Regardless of the criteria selected, school officials must bear in mind that ambiguity is a breeding ground for potential disaster. If a criterion is subject to a wide variety of interpretations, as most criteria are, a dismissal decision may be overturned by the courts on the grounds of insufficient notice. By way of illustration, in ruling in favor of the teacher, a court stated:

> The warning letter ... was totally insufficient.... The letter merely announced very tersely that improvement was needed in the areas of (1) relationship with students, (2) enthusiasm in teaching, (3) disciplinary policies, and (4) relationship with parents. All four charges were so broadly drafted that (the teacher) had no way of knowing exactly how she should improve her conduct.... Without knowledge of the specifics in which classroom conduct is deficient, a teacher who seeks to improve his or her teaching ability may find that such efforts result in classroom conduct that in the minds of school authorities, is even less competent, less efficient.... In short, the teacher is caught in a double-bind; the teacher must improve ... or risk termination. On the other hand, there is no assurance that any particular course of action undertaken by a teacher ... will constitute sufficient improvement in the eyes of the board and school authorities. The teacher finds herself struggling blindly towards *undefined and unknown standards of*

conduct. (*Pollard v. Bd. of Educ. Reorganized School District*, 533 S.W. 2d 667 [1976]; emphasis added)

PROFESSIONAL CONSIDERATIONS

A second approach to setting the criteria for evaluating the effectiveness of a teacher centers on the professional duties of a teacher. Scriven (1988) maintains that a list of job specifications is the only proper basis for evaluating teachers when making personnel decisions. According to him, the professional duties of a teacher are as follows:

1. Knowledge of duties (for example, understanding the curriculum requirements)
2. Knowledge of school and community (including knowledge of local needs and resources)
3. Knowledge of subject matter (knowledge in the fields of special competence and literacy in writing, speaking, and editing)
4. Instructional design (encompasses course design, selection and creation of materials, and competent use of available resources)
5. Gathering information about student achievement (constructing tests, scoring student work, and allocating grades)
6. Providing information about student achievement (for example, gives correct answers, explains the grading standards, and lets students know where they stand in relation to other students)
7. Classroom skills (relating to communication and classroom management)
8. Personal characteristics (ability to accept constructive criticism and to engage in self-evaluation and development)
9. Service to the profession (for example, helping beginners and peers, being knowledgeable about professional issues, and knowing and acting in accordance with the ethics of the profession)

Unlike most writers in the field of teacher evaluation, Scriven distinguishes between criteria (the dimensions along which teaching is assessed) and standards (the level of performance needed to be considered satisfactory). Given the large number of criteria, Scriven asserts that it would be unreasonable to expect a very high level of performance on each of the nine dimensions. He judges it to be more reasonable to expect a minimum level of achievement on every duty and a substantial level of achievement on most. What this exactly means in any given situation depends on the particular circumstances. "However, it is clear that failing certain criteria is essentially unacceptable: communication ability is one of the most important criteria, along with subject matter knowledge, minimal skills of classroom management, test-related skills, and ethics" (Scriven 1988).

SCIENTIFIC CONSIDERATIONS

There is an abundance of research on teaching effectiveness, and this research offers valuable clues to the teacher behaviors that promote student achievement (*see* Gage 1983, Rosenshine 1971, Waxman and Wahlberg 1982). This research can be used as one source for identifying the criteria a district may employ in evaluating its teachers. Users of this research should bear in mind that each of the teacher behaviors exerts a relatively small effect on student achievement in any given school year. However, the cumulative effects of these teacher behaviors over the pupils' school careers will be nontrivial (Gage 1978).

Medley, Coker, and Soar (1984) provide direct access to the findings of this research on teaching effectiveness to those educators who lack the time, inclination, or technical background to locate the relevant studies. These three researchers identify the teaching behaviors that promote student achievement and positive attitudes toward school (for example, using various teaching techniques, dealing with disruptive behavior, and facilitating pupil involvement). For each of these teaching behaviors, the researchers also indicate whether the results are similar or different for pupils of low and high socioeconomic status. Furthermore, these researchers specify what the results are for different grade levels; they cite evidence suggesting that the same teaching behaviors yield opposite results depending on whether the pupils are in the lower or higher grades.

Since most teacher behaviors do not appear to be effective across all types of situations, school districts should be especially careful to select behaviors that match their own situational requirements. The key situational conditions seem to be the grade level and the socioeconomic background of the students.

PRACTICAL CONSIDERATIONS

When choosing the criteria that will be employed in judging the effectiveness of teachers, superintendents also should consider whether it is feasible for supervisors to use these criteria in the evaluation process. For a criterion to be of practical value in evaluating and dismissing tenured teachers for incompetence in the classroom, it should be able to pass three tests.

First, there should be a valid way of determining whether a teacher satisfies the criterion. If there is not, the criterion exists only on paper. One criterion that potentially falls into this category is "knowledge of subject matter." Few, if any, supervisors possess the breadth and depth of knowledge required to evaluate the subject matter competence of teachers in such diverse fields as language, foreign language, mathematics, science, art, and music. This limitation of the supervisor is especially troublesome at a time when the subject matter competence of teachers cannot be taken for granted.

For the past decade, many school districts have faced teacher shortages in certain fields (especially math and science) and confronted the need to lay off teachers due to declining enrollments. Seniority has governed the order of lay-offs in most cases. As a result, teachers have been switched to grade levels or subjects that they have never taught and, perhaps, are only marginally qualified to teach. In light of these responses to admittedly difficult problems, one is hardly surprised to hear Dr. Billy Reagan, former general superintendent of the Houston Independent School District, say, "We will find certainly as much as 25 percent of the teachers in the classrooms of America today that do not possess the skills to teach above the 7th and 8th grade level in terms of content." To prevent the students of these teachers from being shortchanged, school districts need to determine if they have a valid means for judging whether teachers satisfy the criterion of subject matter competence or any other criterion for that matter.

Second, evaluators should be able to specify the indicators they use when attempting to determine if a teacher meets a particular criterion. If supervisors are unable to provide this type of information, their evaluations are apt to be indefensible in a court of law as we have noted. To ensure that its supervisors are able to employ such indicators, a local district may turn to existing research or appraisal instruments that possess empirically demonstrated reliability and validity.

For example, Bush and Kennedy (1977) queried more than 1,000 junior high school students about the specific behaviors of their most lucid teachers. Students judged teachers high on clarity if they did the following: (1) took time when explaining, (2) stressed difficult points, (3) explained new words, (4) gave examples on the board of how to do something, and (5) worked difficult homework problems, selected by students, on the board.

In a similar vein, Evertson and Emmer (1982) list and describe specific indicators of satisfactory classroom discipline based on their year-long observations of effective and ineffective teachers. Teachers who are effective in promoting classroom discipline use the following practices: (1) develop a workable set of rules and procedures; (2) hold students accountable for complying with these rules and procedures; (3) assign reasonable consequences to students who behave inappropriately; and (4) maintain their management system by monitoring student behavior, handling inappropriate behavior promptly, and being consistent in their use of consequences. Concrete examples of these practices, along with the rationale underlying their use, can be found in *Organizing and Managing the Elementary School Classroom* (Evertson and others 1981) and *Organizing and Managing the Junior High Classroom* (Emmer and others 1982).

The Georgia Teacher Performance Assessment Instruments (Capie 1983) contain a wide variety of criteria and their corresponding indicators and descriptors. By way of illustration, the criterion of flexibility and variety is specified as follows:

> *"Demonstrates a repertoire of teaching methods"*
>
> *Indicator 10*—Demonstrates ability to conduct lessons using a variety of teaching methods. Teaching methods such as the following may be observed: drill, inquiry, discussion, role playing, demonstration, explanation, and problem solving.
>
> *Indicator 11*—Demonstrates ability to work with individuals, small groups, and large groups. Group size is matched to the objective; teacher's role is appropriate to each group size being used; transitions from one sized group to another are smooth; different group sizes that are matched to the objectives are used.

Third, supervisors should be able to prescribe remediation if a teacher is found to be deficient with respect to a particular criterion. If supervisors are unable to prescribe appropriate remediation, they may be reluctant to judge the teacher as unsatisfactory. Even if the supervisor is willing to proceed in rating the teacher's performance unsatisfactory, the failure to prescribe remediation is likely to become a fatal legal defect in the district's case against the teacher.

As the foregoing discussion implies, we believe that the selection of criteria demands more than a consideration of what constitutes good teaching. There are numerous legal, professional, scientific, and practical matters to be taken into account. Ideally, these matters should be considered *during* the criterion selection process to avoid the problems we have discussed.

Determine Whether Teachers Satisfy the Criteria

Regardless of the criteria selected by a district to evaluate the effectiveness of its teachers, the next task is to establish sound procedures for determining whether the teachers satisfy each of these criteria. The most important procedural decisions relate to the types of information that will be used in determining whether teachers meet the criteria. These informational sources may be identical across all criteria, or they may vary from one criterion to another. Moreover, districts may choose to employ only one type of information (for example, supervisor ratings) or multiple sources (for example, supervisor ratings and student ratings). The following types of information may be used in evaluating teachers:

1. Supervisor ratings
2. Student ratings
3. Student performance on tests
4. Peer evaluations
5. Self-evaluations
6. Parent ratings
7. Student and parent complaints

The strengths, weaknesses, and legal status of these various types of information are discussed in the remainder of this chapter.

SUPERVISOR RATINGS

The most frequently used source of information for evaluating teachers is supervisor ratings. Although research on these ratings is limited, the following conclusions are consistent with the extant empirical research: (1) supervisory ratings are poor indicators of how much students are learning from teachers, (2) supervisory ratings are unrelated to ratings from other sources, (3) supervisory ratings are ineffective in promoting teacher improvement, and (4) supervisory ratings are accorded great weight by court judges when these ratings are based on classroom observation.

Educational researchers have evinced the greatest interest in studying the relationship between supervisory ratings and measures of pupil achievement. These studies consistently show no relationship between these two indicators of teacher effectiveness; representative conclusions drawn from these studies are as follows:

> The most important finding of this study is the low accuracy of the average principal's judgments of the performance of the teachers he or she supervises. What is particularly striking about the finding is its consistency with the findings of earlier studies (i.e., low correlation between pupil gains in math and reading achievement and principal ratings of the pupils' teachers) (Medley and Coker 1987).
>
> . . . supervisory ratings do not correlate with pupil growth. . . . Perhaps it is a bit unreasonable to expect a supervisor to tell how much a class is learning just by looking at it (Medley and Mitzel 1959).
>
> . . . superintendents, supervisors, and principals tended to rate good teachers low and poor teachers high (goodness defined by pupil growth in achievement).... Ratings by superintendents, supervisors, principals should not be accepted as the sole or valid criteria until persons in these positions have been re-educated for this responsibility (McCall and Krause 1959).
>
> . . . evaluations based on . . . supervisors' ratings and those based on measures of pupil growth and achievement were not significantly correlated (Anderson 1954).
>
> . . . supervisory ratings here provided are invalid (as measures of pupil gain) (LaDuke 1945).
>
> The criterion of pupil change apparently measures something different than that measured by teacher ratings (Gotham 1945).
>
> Whatever pupil gain measures in relation to teaching ability it is not that emphasized in supervisory ratings (R. D. Jones 1946).
>
> Employers' ratings of teaching ability are not related to pupil gains in information (Brookover 1940).
>
> . . . supervisory ratings . . . seem to lack reliability and validity (as measures of pupil gain) (Jayne 1945).

A few empirical studies have examined the relationship between supervisory ratings and ratings from other sources. Supervisory ratings do not appear to be highly or significantly related to student ratings (Brookover 1940, Anderson 1954), peer ratings (Anderson 1954), and self-evaluations by teachers (Anderson 1954, Medley and Mitzel 1959). Principal and parent ratings are modestly related (Epstein 1985). Although there is some mutual recognition of strong and weak teachers, there is considerable disagreement in the ratings of the same teacher by parents and by principals (Epstein 1985).

Even fewer studies have focused on the effectiveness of supervisory ratings in promoting teacher improvement. Tuckman and Oliver (1968) designed an experiment to examine the relative effects of feedback on teachers' behavior. There were four feedback conditions in this study: (l) students only, (2) supervisor (either the principal, vice-principal, or assistant principal) only, (3) students and supervisor, and (4) no feedback. The researchers found that vocational teachers react to feedback, irrespective of source; however, the reaction is negative in the case of feedback from supervisors. These findings prompted the two investigators to conclude that "such feedback is doing more harm than good."

When teachers are questioned about the effectiveness of principal evaluations, teachers tend to view these evaluations as being perfunctory and a necessary evil with little or no impact on actual teaching performance (Kauchak and others 1985). From the teachers' vantage point principal evaluations are an ineffective tool for instructional improvement because they lack rigor, are too brief, occur too infrequently, and are conducted by unknowledgeable principals (Kauchak and others 1985). Somewhat surprisingly, teachers show little hostility to the concept of principal evaluation (Kauchak and others 1985).

Despite the weak empirical support for using supervisor ratings, the courts are inclined to attach great weight to supervisor ratings as long as they are based on adequately documented classroom observations. The following sentiments expressed by one judge reflect this deference to supervisory ratings:

> Teaching is an art as well as a profession and requires a large amount of preparation in order to qualify one in that profession. The ordinary layman is not well versed in that art, neither is he in a position to measure the necessary qualifications required for the teacher of today. In our judgment this information can be imparted by one who is versed and alert in the profession and aware of the qualifications required.... We think *the principal with the years of experience possessed by him can be classed properly as an expert in the teaching profession, and is in a similar position as a doctor in the medical profession.* (*Fowler v. Young et al., Board of Education*, 65 N.E. 2d 399 [1945]; emphasis added)

Another judge expressed his regard for supervisory ratings based on classroom observations even more pointedly and succinctly:

> The court below seems to have relied principally upon the testimony of those who have actually observed the teaching of ap-

pellant.... This testimony was sufficient in itself to support the court's conclusion (to uphold the school board's dismissal decision). (*Appeal of Mulhollen*, 39 A. 2d 283 [1944])

STUDENT RATINGS

At the college level student ratings are commonly used to evaluate the effectiveness of classroom instruction (Aleamoni 1981). Over the past fifty years extensive research has been conducted on the reliability and validity of these ratings. This body of research provides strong empirical support for the following conclusions: (l) student ratings are highly stable (Aleamoni 1981), (2) they are strongly related to student achievement (Cohen 1981), and (3) they are highly effective in promoting improvement within a class over the course of a semester (Cohen 1981). This research leaves no doubt that student ratings represent a sound choice for evaluating instruction at the college level.

Although research on the reliability and validity of student ratings at the elementary and secondary levels of education is much more sparse, the results are generally consistent with what has been found at the college level. Student ratings appear to be reliable (Fox and others 1983, Bryan 1963, Remers 1939, and Stalnecker and Remers 1929) and highly related to teacher behavior assessments made by trained observers (Fox and others 1983). Similarly, student ratings are effective in fostering changes in teacher behavior and instructional improvement (Bryan 1963, Gage and others 1960, Tuckman and Oliver 1968). Finally, student ratings are reasonably good indicators of how much students are learning from their teachers. In the most carefully designed and comprehensive study on this issue, McCall and Krause (1959) conclude, "The only persons in the school system who were found to be professionally competent to judge the worth (as measured by gains in achievement) of teachers were their pupils." Three other studies (Eash and others 1980, Anderson 1954, and Lins 1946) show low, but positive, correlations between student ratings of teacher effectiveness and pupil growth in achievement. On balance, the empirical case that can be made for student ratings is much stronger than the one that can be made for supervisor ratings.

When teachers are queried about the value of student evaluations, they express three different positions in relatively equal numbers (Kauchak and others 1985). Teachers who are positive toward the use of student evaluations stress the amount of time exposure as crucial to their value. However, in expressing their approval of such evaluations, teachers carefully limit the topics to be evaluated to what they like about the teacher and the class. Teachers do not believe that students are capable of making judgments about instructional competence. Teachers who are skeptical of the value of student evaluations underscore the inability of students to differentiate between good and popular teachers. Those teachers who oppose the use of student evaluations focus on the inability of students to understand the complexities of teaching and the possible influence of emotions on these evaluations. In general, elementary teachers are less favorable toward student evaluations than high school teachers.

The legal status of student ratings, unlike that of supervisor ratings, is inconclusive, however. Only one of the tenured dismissal cases examined by Bridges and Gumport (1984) mentioned the use of student ratings. In this particular case the judge disregarded the ratings because they were gathered after it became public knowledge that the principal was dissatisfied with the teacher's performance and intended to fire her. Understandably the judge reasoned that the students' ratings may have been biased against the teacher as they were influenced by the actions of the principal. Since the judge did not object to the use of student ratings per se, school officials probably can employ them in dismissal cases as partial evidence of a teacher's incompetence. Resting a case solely on this source of appraisal is inadvisable because students are not trained to act as evaluators (in this sense they are laymen).

STUDENT TEST RESULTS

Student test results, like supervisor and student ratings, may be used for purposes of formative evaluation (that is, to improve instruction) or summative evaluation (that is, to make decisions about the employment status of teachers). When used for formative purposes, there is some evidence that student test results can lead to instructional improvement. However, when test results are used for summative purposes, the picture is somewhat mixed. Research shows that (1) teachers strongly oppose the use of student test results for summative purposes; (2) overemphasis on student test results leads to teacher stress and cheating; and (3) the courts are inclined to view student test results as defensible indicators of a teacher's effectiveness as long as certain conditions are met.

Under certain conditions, student test results stimulate instructional growth and improvement. The most beneficial outcomes occur when principals meet with individual teachers or with groups of teachers to discuss patterns of students' test results (Kennedy 1983). Following such discussion, teachers attempt to discover their instructional strengths and weaknesses and to make appropriate modifications in their teaching practices. This consultative approach to the use of student test results appears to be relatively stress-free for teachers. They report learning a great deal during this process and acquiring a greater sense of the best ways to teach.

When student test results are used for summative purposes, the reactions of teachers are overwhelmingly negative. In a recent study (Kauchak and others 1985), the responses were so strong and uniformly against the practice that questions concerning the use of achievement scores to evaluate teachers were eventually dropped. Opposition to the practice centered around two positions. Teachers either questioned the validity of standardized achievement tests for assessing student performance or questioned the validity of such tests as measures of teaching performance. When asked to rate the suitability of various methods for evaluating teachers, they assigned the lowest rating to the use of achievement tests.

Those districts that ignore the objections of teachers and use student test results to evaluate the effectiveness of the teaching staff find that test scores rise. However, the increases are accompanied by high levels of anxiety and cheating by teachers (Kennedy 1983, Stringfield and Hartman 1985).

Teacher cheating to raise the test scores takes several forms: encouraging bilingual and low-ability students to be absent when the test is administered; getting a copy of the test and teaching students to answer its specific items; and teaching to the brighter students since they can raise the class average on the test. Administrators in these districts often erroneously assumed that higher test scores reflected increased student learning (Kennedy 1983).

If a district decides to use test scores to assess the effectiveness of its teaching staff, it should use a variety of measures to detect and discourage cheating (Stringfield and Hartman 1985). Promising devices to detect the possibility of cheating include (1) the existence of large discrepancies (15 or more points) between grades within the same school; (2) the presence of large differences in subtest scores within the same classroom; and (3) large gains by a student cohort one year followed by a large drop the next year. To prevent cheating school district officials should change tests (or use alternating forms) every year, monitor the testing procedures rigorously, and retest frequently.

Although there are reasonable grounds for questioning the use of student test results for summative purposes, such results appear to be a legally defensible means of evaluating teacher effectiveness. The reasoning of one judge is instructive on this admittedly controversial matter:

> Passing judgment on the level of disruption in a classroom and the level of competency of a teacher of necessity presents a situation where reliance upon subjective perceptions is unavoidable, but *when seemingly objective uniform test results are available they should be considered*. (*In the Matter of Joseph McCrum v. Board of Education of the New York City School District*, 396 N.Y.S. 2d 691[1977]; emphasis added)

At least one teacher (nontenured) has been dismissed for incompetence solely on the grounds of student test scores. The teacher contested the board's use of low scores on the Iowa Tests of Basic Skills and the Iowa Tests of Educational Development as a violation of her Fourteenth Amendment rights. The trial court ruled that a teacher's professional competence could not be determined solely on the basis of her students' achievement on these tests, especially where students maintain normal educational growth rates. However, the Court of Appeals overturned the lower court decision and stated in its ruling:

> Such matters as the competence of teachers, and the standards of its measurement are not . . . matters of constitutional dimensions. They are peculiarly appropriate to state and local administration. (*Scheelhaase v. Woodbury Central Community School District*, 488 F. 2d 237 [1973])

Since the evidence on the legality of student tests is limited, school districts are well advised to use these results only if the following conditions are met. First, dismissal solely on the grounds of poor student test performance should be considered only when this poor performance is repeated over a period of at least two or three years. The effects of teachers on different groups of students are relatively unstable (that is, inconsistent) from one year to the next; these effects are even unstable from one topic to another for the *same* students (Rosenshine 1977). In light of this instability, it would be unfair to dismiss teachers for incompetence because their students performed poorly on an achievement test in a single year. Second, the district should rely only on achievement tests that reflect the prescribed curriculum (Haertel 1986); accordingly, standardized achievement tests should be avoided because they are likely to be a poor match with the curriculum (Millman 1981). Third, school districts should rule out the possibility that the relatively poor performance of a teacher's students is due to initial differences in the performance potential of the students (Haertel 1986).

PEER EVALUATIONS

There are relatively few studies of peer evaluations for either formative or summative purposes. In the studies that have been conducted, the following trends are evident: (1) peer evaluations do not appear to be a regular component of districtwide systems for evaluating teachers (Bridges and Gumport 1984, Kowalski 1978); (2) teachers generally react positively to the idea of being evaluated by other teachers (Kauchak and others 1985, McCarthey and Peterson 1988); (3) teachers who serve as peer evaluators are positive about their experiences and indicate a willingness to serve in this capacity again (Benzley and others 1985, Pfeifer 1987); (4) peer evaluations, like supervisory ratings, are poor indicators of pupil growth in achievement as measured by tests (Anderson 1954, McCall and Krause 1959); (5) there are some promising models of collegial evaluation (Roper and Hoffman 1986) but the reliability and effectiveness of peer evaluations in stimulating instructional improvement remain unknown and unstudied; and (6) peer ratings are legally defensible but rarely figure in tenure dismissal cases (Bridges and Gumport 1984).

Teachers generally react positively to the idea of being evaluated by other teachers when these peer evaluators come from the same subject area or grade level (Kauchak and others 1985). This receptivity extends to peer evaluations based on review of teaching materials (for example, course outlines, syllabi, tests, and homework), as well as classroom visitations (Kauchak and others 1985, McCarthey and Peterson 1988). When teachers express reservations about the practice, they center around the potential disturbance of professional relations within the school. To minimize the potential for such problems, teachers suggest that peer evaluators be recruited from different schools.

Those teachers who have actually served as peer evaluators also endorse the practice. In the study by Benzley, Kauchak, and Peterson (1985) the vast majority of peer evaluators indicated that they would participate again if asked. They reported that their involvement generated new ideas about teaching and made them more aware of the ways in which they taught. Contrary to expectations, serving as a peer evaluator did not create problems with other teachers. When problems arose, they related to finding qualified substitutes for those teachers who were acting as peer evaluators.

Although the usefulness of peer evaluations in stimulating instructional improvement has not been established, this form of evaluation is currently being advocated by those who support the professionalization of teaching. One promising approach to the use of collegial evaluation for instructional improvement is the Stanford Collegial Evaluation Program (Roper and Hoffman 1986). The heart of this program is a dyad; two teachers take turns in enacting the roles of evaluator and evaluatee. The Stanford Program has seven interdependent steps: (1) choosing a partner; (2) selecting criteria; (3) self-assessment; (4) evaluation by students; (5) observation by a peer; (6) conferences; and (7) planning a program of improvement. Roper and Hoffman (1986) describe each of these steps fully and offer useful insights into this process by drawing on the results of their field test.

Legally, peer evaluations, whether they are based on classroom observation or documentation, are apt to withstand judicial scrutiny. Peers, like supervisors, are trained professionals who presumably are well versed in the art and science of teaching. The use of peers to evaluate the research accomplishments of professors is an established practice in colleges and universities and has never been questioned by the courts as a lawful practice. Although the practice has never been widespread in school districts, the decision of the Toledo, Ohio, district to base the dismissal of probationary teachers for incompetence primarily on evaluations by teachers may be the harbinger of a revolution in teacher evaluation procedures. In this district, approximately 10 percent of the probationary teachers have been dismissed upon the recommendation of peers over the past years. To our knowledge the validity of this practice has not been contested in the courts.

SELF-EVALUATIONS

Educational researchers have exhibited little interest in studying self-evaluations, that is, teacher ratings of their own performance. The studies that have been conducted reveal the following trends: (1) less than 10 percent of the districts in the United States report self-evaluation as a component of their evaluation system (National Education Association 1969); (2) teachers are not accurate reporters of their own behavior in the classroom; (3) self-evaluations under certain conditions promote instructional improvement; and (4) self-evaluations are of limited value for summative purposes.

When self-evaluations have been studied, most of the studies have concentrated on the accuracy of teacher reports of their own behavior in the classroom. In these studies, teachers have been asked to report on the percentage of class time spent in teacher talk; the extent to which they rely on various teaching methods (for example, discussion, lecture, and recitation); and the extent to which they use such activities as individualized instruction. When these teacher self-reports of specific behaviors are correlated with the reports of trained observers, there are discrepancies between what teachers believe to be happening and what they actually do in their classrooms. In none of the half-dozen studies reviewed by Hook and Rosenshine (1979) is there any correspondence between reported practice and observed behavior. The reviewers conclude, "One is not advised to accept teacher reports of specific behaviors as particularly accurate."

Self-evaluations may be used to promote instructional improvement. Hoover and Carroll (1987) have developed an effective approach for improving the quality of reading instruction at the elementary level. In their program, teachers are provided with the opportunity to assess their teaching effectiveness by using a checklist to analyze audiotapes of their own reading instruction. This checklist focuses on those teaching practices that research shows are effective in fostering student achievement in reading (for example, lesson begins with a signal and an overview, children are called on individually, and specific, rather than general, praise is used). Teachers learn about this research and its limitations prior to using the checklist. They are encouraged to decide for themselves whether they wish to change their practices in light of the research and the analysis of their own reading instruction. Most teachers chose to modify their instruction in line with the recommended practices.

For those who are interested in using a similar approach to improving instruction at the high school level, the Low Inference Self-Assessment Measure (LISAM) developed by Freiberg (1987) is worth considering. LISAM can be used by teachers to analyze audiotapes of their classroom teaching along the following dimensions: questioning techniques, teacher and student talk, wait-time, praise, use of student ideas, and strategies for achieving closure. Freiberg, like Hoover and Carroll, chose these teaching practices based on research.

Self-evaluations can also be combined with student feedback to produce positive changes in teacher behavior. In an ambitious study Gage and others (1960) conducted an experiment to examine the effect of student feedback on teacher behavior. As part of this study, teachers described themselves on a teacher behavior questionnaire and indicated how they would be described by their pupils. The students provided two descriptions—how their ideal teacher would behave and how their teacher actually behaved. The results were fed back to teachers. The feedback led to changes in the teachers' behavior and produced improvement in the accuracy of teachers' perceptions of their pupils' opinions. Somewhat surprisingly, the teacher behavior questionnaires focused the attention of teachers on their classroom behaviors and led to behavior changes even when the teacher did not receive the feedback from students.

When confidential self-evaluations by teachers are related to their students' gains in achievement, the results are mixed. Two studies (McCall and Krause 1959, Medley and Mitzel 1959) indicate that elementary teachers are fair judges of their own effectiveness in teaching pupils to read. A third study (Anderson 1954) shows a negative relationship between teacher self-evaluations and student achievement gains.

Thus far, official self-evaluations have not figured in the dismissal cases of tenured teachers for incompetence (Bridges and Gumport 1984). In light of the tendency of teachers to overrate themselves (Rippey 1981) and the conflict of interest involved in such ratings, it is unlikely that self-evaluations will be used for summative purposes. One possible exception may be in states like Kansas that specify, "Persons to be evaluated should participate in their evaluations, including an opportunity for self-evaluation." Even in states like Kansas, the requirement of self-evaluation could perhaps be met by limiting its role to evaluation for formative purposes, that is, the improvement of instruction.

PARENT EVALUATIONS

Parents can be viewed as organizational "outsiders" or as "members" of the organizational community (Corwin and Wagenaar 1976). As "members," parents have a stake in the success and improvement of schools and are in a position to know when teachers make special efforts to assist their children in attaining basic or advanced skills (Epstein 1985). Accordingly, parents are potentially important judges of teacher and school effectiveness. Studies of parental roles in the evaluation process are scarce, however.

In the one study that has examined parent evaluations of teachers, Epstein (1985) explored how the evaluations from this source related to principal ratings and student achievement. The correlation between principal and parent ratings is modest.

> There is some mutual recognition of strong and weak teachers, but also considerable disagreement in the ratings of the same teacher by parents and by principals. (Epstein 1985)

Neither principal nor parent ratings were associated with the teachers' reports of average classroom achievement of students in reading and math.

Parents give high marks to teachers who frequently engage in the

following activities:
1. involve parents in learning activities at home
2. provide parents with ideas on how they might help their child at home
3. let parents know about the instructional program
4. encourage parents to help their child at home
5. work hard to interest and excite parents

These results indicate that parents, when given an opportunity to evaluate teachers, relate teacher performance to the resources and ideas that the teacher offers parents. Moreover, there is evidence in this study that principals tend to overlook these teacher qualities.

Including all parents in the evaluation process may remove some of the bias in the reports principals typically receive from parents (Epstein 1985). When the reports from many parents are aggregated, they provide a relatively stable rating of the teachers' effectiveness in promoting parent involvement in their children's education. By systematically using the assessments of all parents, school officials can minimize the effect of one or two vocal and disgruntled parents on a teacher's performance evaluation.

To this date, formal evaluations of teachers by parents have not figured in any tenured dismissal cases; therefore, the legal status of parent evaluations is unclear. If a district chooses to use such evaluations in dismissal cases, it is advisable for district officials to take two steps. First, parents should be asked to evaluate only those aspects of a teacher's performance that the parent is in a position to observe. The five activities listed earlier fall into this category. Second, school district officials should not base a dismissal case solely on parent evaluations; supervisor evaluations based on classroom observations are needed for the case to pass judicial scrutiny.

STUDENT AND PARENT COMPLAINTS

In the absence of an organizational approach like the one described in this monograph, teacher evaluation is apt to be complaint-driven (Bridges 1989). That is to say, administrators are likely to ignore poorly performing teachers unless there are complaints from students and parents. Complaints are most likely to prompt administrative action if there are lots of them and the complainants describe quite specifically what happened and when it occurred (Bridges 1990). When complaints arise and the district lacks an organizational approach to teacher evaluation, the teacher is apt to be transferred to schools where parents are unlikely to complain. These schools are usually attended by minority students from lower social class backgrounds (Bridges 1989 and 1990).

To encourage the voicing of complaints by students and parents from lower, as well as middle and upper, social classes, the Salt Lake City, Utah, school district has incorporated a formal complaint process into its teacher evaluation system. If a student or parent is unable to resolve a grievance satisfactorily with the person against whom the complaint is lodged, the disgruntled student or parent may file a written request for a "Review of Services." Over the past decade one-third of all the teachers who have been placed on remediation in that district have been identified through the "Review of Services" process.

Although most districts have not formalized such a process for filing complaints, student and parent complaints frequently figure in dismissal cases of tenured teachers for incompetence (Bridges and Gumport 1984). Such complaints legitimately can be used to provide the necessary background for understanding the performance deficiencies of a teacher. However, conclusions about the competence of a teacher that are based solely or mainly on the complaints of students and parents are likely to be viewed as ill-founded. In the words of one court,

> While it is not the function nor the desire of courts to second-guess school boards, nevertheless, it is clear that our *Legislature has intended to grant to tenured teachers some protection from ... disgruntled parents*.... There *is* little doubt that Mrs. Schulz might do herself a favor by being less rigid.... (She) is "an old-fashioned teacher." Perhaps such teachers do not win popularity contests, but neither can they be said to be incompetent. They are not required to entertain their students, only to teach them. (*Schulz v. Board of Education of the School District of Fremont*, 315 N.W. 2d 633 [1982]; emphasis added)

Supervisory evaluations of this teacher based on classroom observations were "above average" and were accorded substantially greater weight by the Court of Appeals.

IMPLICATIONS

When deciding what sources and types of information to use in evaluating the effectiveness of teachers, school officials have no single alternative that is completely satisfactory. If evaluation is to be used for formative purposes, there are four reasonable alternatives: using student ratings at the midpoint of the semester or year, training teachers to analyze audiotapes of their own classroom instruction, having teachers evaluate one another, and using the results of curriculum-valid tests to explore where instruction is apparently weak and how it might be improved.

If evaluation is to be used for summative purposes and to build a legally defensible case, districts should use evaluations based on classroom observations by expert supervisors. When supervisory ratings are used, a school district is well advised to base termination decisions on evaluations conducted by more than one supervisor for at least two reasons. First, the composite ratings of two or more supervisors are somewhat more reliable and valid than the ratings based on a single source (Gotham 1945, Brookover 1940). Second, while there may be "no statutory duty to have more than one person conducting the evaluations, the severity of termination for a tenured teacher suggests that such a course be wise" (*Ganyo v. Independent School District No. 832*, 311 N.W. 2d 497 [1981]). In addition to relying on more than one supervisor's judgments of a teacher's effectiveness in the classroom, a school district should consider using other sources and types of information as well. Student ratings, peer evaluations, parent and student complaints, and parent evaluations represent viable possibilities. Even though achievement test results are legally defensible under the conditions we have noted, they generally are poor choices because of teachers' responses to the use of such tests for summative purposes.

4

Provide Appropriate Remediation

Tenured teachers are entitled to have an opportunity to correct their deficiencies if their shortcomings are deemed remediable (Claxton 1986). The reasons for this entitlement are succinctly stated by the Washington Supreme Court:

> When a teacher is discharged because of classroom deficiencies, the consequences are severe. Chances of other employment in the profession are diminished, if not eliminated. Much time and money has been expended by the teacher in obtaining the requisite credentials. It would be manifestly unfair to allow a discharge for a teaching or classroom deficiency which is reasonably correctable. (*Wojt v. Chimacum School District*, 9 Wash. App. 857, 516 P.2d 1099 [1973])

In determining whether a teacher's conduct is remediable, some courts have used the following standard:

> (1) no permanent damage has been done to the students, faculty or school; (2) the teacher could have corrected the deficiency had she been warned by school administrators; and (3) the conduct has not existed over such a long period of time so as to have become irremediable. (Claxton 1986)

Discipline and control problems that are common among incompetent teachers are considered remediable by the courts. Character faults (for example, male teachers who caress female students) and abhorrent crimes such as rape are deemed irremediable (Claxton 1986).

Although remediation is a legally mandated right of a tenured teacher, the remediation process is seldom successful (Bridges 1990). "At risk" teachers rarely show improvement during this process. The failure of remediation for veteran teachers is due to several reasons. Administrators lack knowledge and skill in identifying the causes for a teacher's poor performance and in prescribing the appropriate types of remediation. Moreover, incompetent teachers often resist efforts to improve their performance. Having been fed a steady diet of satisfactory evaluations in the past, they are inclined to view negative evaluations and remedial efforts as unwarranted (Bridges 1990). Their resistance and defensiveness, though somewhat understandable, are not conducive to improved performance.

To assist school officials in designing remedial efforts that are more likely to succeed than fail, we shall focus on three important aspects of remediation—the causes of poor performance, the types of remediation, and the length of the remediation period. In our judgment, a sound program of remediation must address all three aspects.

CAUSES OF POOR PERFORMANCE

Before supervisors choose the types of remediation to be used in improving a teacher's performance, they must endeavor to understand the causes of the unsatisfactory performance; otherwise, the types of remediation that they choose may be directed at the wrong target. Steinmetz (1969) suggests that there are three major causes of unsatisfactory performance: (1) managerial and/or organizational shortcomings, (2) a problem with the employee, and (3) outside or non-job-related influences affecting the employee. Any one or a combination of these three causes may be the root of the teacher's poor performance in the classroom.

The managerial and/or organizational shortcomings that may contribute to incompetent teaching are fairly numerous. Perhaps the most prevalent type of managerial shortcoming is related to the criteria for judging the effectiveness of teachers; supervisors in educational organizations often fail to communicate the criteria they use when evaluating teachers (Natriello and Dornbusch 1980-81). Teachers also may perform poorly because they have been changed to a teaching assignment that they are not properly trained to handle. Likewise, teachers may be experiencing difficulty because they have too many preparations, too many "difficult" students, or too few resources.

A second major cause of unsatisfactory performance in the classroom is an individual shortcoming of the teacher. He or she may not be motivated to perform at a satisfactory level and simply fails to expend the effort necessary to be a competent teacher. Poor performance also may stem from a lack of skill or ability; the teacher is perhaps willing, but unable, to carry out one or more of his or her teaching tasks in a satisfactory manner. Personal pathologies may also account for the teacher's difficulties in the classroom. He or she may be suffering from alcoholism, drug addiction, mental illness, or serious emotional distress.

The third major cause of unsatisfactory performance is an outside influence. The teacher may be having problems in the classroom due to problems outside the workplace. These outside problems may be marital difficulties, conflicts with children, or financial problems.

Since teachers may not be dismissed for problems that are due to managerial or organizational shortcomings, supervisors must overcome their tendencies to ignore shortcomings emanating from these sources. Moreover, supervisors need to determine what the causes might be if appropriate ameliorative measures are to be taken. The types of remediation to be employed should reflect to some extent the perceived causes of the teacher's difficulties.

TYPES OF REMEDIATION

There are basically ten types of remediation that may be used to improve the teacher's classroom teaching performance. These ten types are as follows: goal setting, instructional input, modeling, practice, feedback, coaching, reinforcement, therapy, counseling, and environmental change.

Goal setting apparently leads to improved performance (Latham and Wexley 1981) if it clarifies exactly what is expected of the employee. The way in which goals are set is less important than the act of setting a specific goal. Goals assigned unilaterally by a supervisor seem to be as effective as goals arrived at jointly by the supervisor and the employee. Hard goals are more effective than moderate or easy goals. Ordinarily, these goals should be set in relation to the teacher's deficiencies in meeting the district's criteria for effective teaching.

Instructional input refers to the information and knowledge the teacher receives in relation to a particular skill. This information can be presented in the form of books or articles to read, films to view, and courses or workshops to attend. The content for remediation plans can be selected from those options that promise substantial increases in student learning (Joyce and others 1987). There are numerous options, including cooperative learning (Slavin 1983, Cohen 1986), teaching strategies that assist students in organizing information for mastery (Stone 1983), and specific teaching practices that facilitate student achievement if used regularly (for example, "wait time" formulated by Rowe [1974], "Teacher Expectations" developed by Kerman [1979], and "Mastery Learning" conceived by Bloom [1984] and elaborated by Block [1975]).

Modeling allows the teacher to observe examples of a teaching performance that exemplifies key behaviors and skills. Modeling may be limited to positive examples, or it may consist of contrasting negative and positive examples. Usually modeling is used to introduce complex or otherwise unfamiliar behavior. There are several ways in which the teacher can be supplied with models—opportunities to visit and observe the classrooms of exceptional teachers, staged demonstrations in the problem teacher's own classroom by outstanding teachers, team teaching assignments with gifted teachers, and opportunities to view videotapes of effective classroom teaching practices.

An excellent videotape on classroom management, a common problem for incompetent teachers, is *Setting the Tone* (Rosenberg 1987). This highly creative and useful training tape features eight elementary, middle, and secondary school teachers on their first day of school. Each of these teachers has an effective, but contrasting, method of establishing the classroom climate for the rest of the school year.

Practice provides the teacher with an opportunity to try out the new behavior or skill in a restricted environment before attempting to incorporate the practice in his or her own classroom. Role playing and microteaching represent two possibilities for providing teachers with practice opportunities. It is estimated that a teacher needs to practice a model of teaching from ten to twenty times in simulated settings if transfer to the actual classroom is to occur (Joyce and Showers 1981).

Feedback is information about past behavior presented to the person who performed that behavior. In remediation, feedback may be provided to the teacher in connection with opportunities for practice or observations of the teacher's performance during the period of remediation. Feedback that is a direct measure of performance is more effective than feedback that is the result of another person's judgment about performance (Miller 1978). Direct feedback can be provided in a number of ways. The teacher can listen to an audiotape recording or view a videotape of his or her own classroom performance. If the teacher is threatened by these technologies, the supervisor can provide a written record of what was said by the teacher and the students during a classroom teaching episode or use a classroom seating chart to report information about the nature of the teacher's verbal interaction with students (for example, teacher questions, student answers, teacher praise, and student questions).

Coaching facilitates the transfer of training and is "characterized by an observation and feedback cycle in an ongoing instructional or clinical situation" (Joyce and Showers 1981). This type of remediation assists teachers in integrating instructional skills or strategies into their own classroom teaching. Feedback stresses the appropriateness of specific strategies to certain goals. "Together, the teacher and 'coach' examine appropriate places in the curriculum for the use of specific strategies, evaluate the effectiveness of observed lessons, and plan for future trials" (Joyce and Showers 1981).

Reinforcement is anything that strengthens or maintains the frequency and duration of behavior. There are several types of reinforcers. Social reinforcers consist of attention paid by others; this attention may come in the form of praise, thanks, appreciation, and smiles. Intrinsic reinforcers occur as the natural result of the work itself; a person experiences pride or satisfaction from the newly acquired behavior. Tangible reinforcers consist of concrete objects such as pay, promotion, and other material rewards. Since reinforcement is defined from the perspective of the recipient rather than of the provider, supervisors cannot assume that what is desirable from their point of view will be a reinforcement for the employee. Rewards become reinforcement only if they strengthen or maintain behavior (Miller 1978)!

Therapy refers to treatment programs that have been designed to deal with specific personal disorders. These therapeutic programs may focus on individual pathologies like alcoholism, drug abuse, and mental illness. Alcoholics Anonymous is one example of these treatment programs.

Counseling is a professional service that is designed to assist the employee in dealing with crisis situations and personal problems that may interfere with his or her performance on the job. Toledo's Employee Assistance Program offers counseling to help teachers cope more effectively with their own personal difficulties and is an example of this type of remediation.

Environmental change refers to modifications that are made in the situational context in which the employee works. Environmental change may be accomplished in a variety of ways: reassign the teacher to another grade level or subject area; reduce the number of preparations which the teacher has; transfer the teacher to another supervisor or building; and provide the teacher with a greater variety of instructional materials.

In selecting the types of remediation that are appropriate for a particular teacher, the supervisor should take into account the causes for the poor performance. The effectiveness of remediation depends to a large extent on matching the cause with the type of remediation that is targeted to that cause. Figure 1 contains five possible configurations of the causes for poor performance and the types of remediation. For example, configuration 1 identifies the cause of a teacher's poor performance as a managerial or organizational shortcoming and prescribes two types of remediation—goal setting and environmental change. Configuration 4, on the other hand, indicates that the teacher's poor performance is due to a personal disorder like alcoholism or substance abuse and prescribes goal setting, therapy, feedback, and reinforcement.

Figure 1. Types of Remediation by Cause

Causes of Poor Performance

Type of Remediation	Managerial Shortcomings (1)	Personal Shortcomings — Motivational (2)	Personal Shortcomings — Skill (3)	Disorder (4)	Outside Influences (5)
Goal setting	•	•		•	•
Instructional input			•		
Modeling			•		
Practice			•		
Feedback		•	•	•	•
Coaching			•		
Reinforcement		•		•	•
Therapy				•	
Counseling					•
Environmental change	•				

If the underlying cause for a teacher's substandard performance is a personal shortcoming, namely, a skill deficiency, research on the effectiveness of inservice training indicates that performance can be improved by using a combination of five types of remediation (Joyce and Showers 1980). These types are *instructional input* (presentation of theory or description of skill or strategy), *modeling* (demonstrations of skills or models of teaching), *practice* (rehearsal of the skill in a simulated setting), structured and open-ended *feedback* (information about performance), and *coaching* (assistance in integrating the skill or strategy into the teacher's classroom teaching). Coaching appears to be somewhat less effective in improving teaching performance than the other four types of remediation, however (Wade 1984-1985).

LENGTH OF REMEDIATION

The duration of a remediation period may be specified in state statutes; if so, the length of remediation is likely to be 90 days. Whenever the period is fixed by statute, school officials may not shorten it. On the other hand, if the state statutes are silent on this issue, school officials should provide the teacher with a reasonable period in which to improve. What is reasonable depends upon the facts and circumstances in each case as the following example suggests:

> The teacher, by statute, must be given a reasonable time in which to correct the deficiencies outlined. Considering this teacher's 17 years of service in the district, in addition to 8 years of teaching elsewhere, it seems harsh and unreasonable to accord her only 5 weeks after the notice of deficiency before the first observation and 8 weeks before the notice of termination to remedy 25 years of teaching practice which was now labeled deficient for the first time. (*Joy Ganyo v. Independent School District*, No. 832, 311 N.W. 2d 497 [1981])

Some of the relevant facts appear to be total years of teaching service, length of service in the district, and the quality of the teacher's performance during this time period.

In determining whether the remediation has been successful, school officials may conduct assessments of the teacher's performance during the remediation period, afterwards, or both. The timing of these assessments is an absolutely critical feature of the district's case against a teacher as this statement by an Illinois appellate court attests:

> ... we believe it was incumbent on the Board in this case to ground its dismissal decisions on observations and evaluations made *after*, and not during the remediation period. Observations during the remediation period could be properly used to evaluate improvement but the absence of any evaluation at the conclusion of the period made it impossible for the Board to make a reasoned decision. (*Board of Education of School District No. 131 v. Illinois State Board of Education*, 403 N.E. 2d 277 [1980])

In a few instances, the teacher will improve during the remediation period and will be rated satisfactory at its conclusion. Following this period of remediation, the teacher may begin to backslide and to manifest some or all of his or her previous deficiencies. This reversal may lead to a situation in which the teacher receives a second unsatisfactory rating. Is the teacher entitled to a second period of remediation before dismissal? The answer appears to be no; a Pennsylvania court issued the following ruling on this matter:

> ... if there is an acceptable rating in between the two unsatisfactory ratings, one can only conclude that the employee cannot or will not maintain the level of performance that is continuously required. The Secretary (of Education) properly found that there was substantial evidence to support the finding of "incompetency." (*Grant D. Steffen v. Board of Directors of South Middletown Township School District*, Pa. Cmwlth., 377 A 2d 1381 [1977])

The court went on to note that the interval between unsatisfactory ratings could be of such duration that the second unsatisfactory rating should not result in dismissal. A three-year interval appears to be the longest period after which the second unsatisfactory rating should result in dismissal.

The issue of backsliding also figured in an Illinois tenure case. In addressing this issue, the court stated:

> We have read in detail the evidence in this case.... The record here demonstrates that this teacher during the period would appear to improve and then back-slide into his previous habits.... We fully recognize that the Teacher Tenure Law has as its benign purpose job security for worthy teachers and serves as a protective shield against dismissal for trivial, political, capricious or arbitrary causes. It was not intended to lock a teacher into a school system where efforts over a period of years by the administration to help the teacher fail to sustain satisfactory performance.... There is substantial evidence in the record to support the conclusion that his period of usefulness in this particular district had waned or perhaps completely evaporated. (*Theodore Kallas v. Board of Education of Marshall Community Unit School District No. C-2, Clark County*, 304 N.E. 2d 527 [1973])

This case, as well as the one in Pennsylvania, suggests that teachers are not entitled to remediation in perpetuity.

In this section, we have discussed three elements of a systematic approach to remediation. A critical feature of this approach is the supervisor's ability to pinpoint the underlying cause of a teacher's poor performance and to prescribe the types of remediation that are appropriate to the perceived cause of the teacher's classroom difficulties. Since supervisors are predisposed to attribute a poor performance to internal rather than external causes, the possibility of a misdiagnosis or a faulty attribution is ever present. This matter is treated extensively in the next section under the heading "ability to diagnose."

5

Ensure That Supervisors Have the Requisite Competencies

Evaluation of teaching competence with a view toward possible dismissal requires special knowledge and skills that are frequently overlooked in the preservice preparation of school administrators. Specifically, the administrator needs to possess the following abilities and knowledge if he or she is to perform evaluation responsibilities effectively:

1. the ability to describe and analyze what is happening in a teacher's classroom
2. the ability to provide an unbiased rating of a teacher's performance
3. the ability to diagnose the cause(s) for a teacher's poor performance
4. the ability to prescribe remediation that is appropriate to the teacher's classroom deficiencies
5. the ability to conduct conferences with teachers regarding their instructional performance
6. the ability to document matters related to 1 through 5
7. knowledge of the legal bases for evaluating and dismissing incompetent teachers

Since these related skills and knowledge are seldom emphasized in university programs for preparing school administrators, local districts need to take steps to ensure that their evaluators possess these skills. Before discussing what these steps might be, let us focus our attention on the skills themselves.

COMPETENCIES

Ability to describe and analyze. If appraisers are going to base their evaluations, wholly or in part, on classroom observations, they need to be able to select (1) *a focus* for their observation and (2) *a technique* for gathering the observational data. Because a major objective of classroom instruction is to determine whether a teacher meets the district's criteria for judging the competence of its teaching force, these data must be targeted to the criteria. If a teacher is not meeting one or more of the criteria, an important related objective of the observation is to provide a written record of the events in the classroom that led the appraiser to conclude that a teacher was failing to satisfy a particular criterion.

The focus of the classroom observation may be on one or more of the following: teacher behaviors, instructional activities, teaching processes, or student responses. Teacher behaviors represent a relatively narrow focus and should be specific enough that a low level of inference is entailed in determining whether they are present or absent. For example, if a district employs clarity in imparting subject matter as a criterion of teaching effectiveness, the evaluator should focus his observations on such specific teaching behaviors as "gives examples," "defines new words," and "has students work sample problems under her supervision before allowing students to work on their own."

Instructional activities relate to a somewhat broader set of events within the classroom and span a longer time period. The most common types of instructional activities are large group (lecture and recitation), small group (discussion and cooperative learning), and individual (seatwork and tutoring). If an appraiser is interested in whether a teacher has met the criterion of flexibility and variety, the focus of the observation can be on the frequency with which the teacher uses these various activities.

A focus on instructional processes involves an integrated, as opposed to a segmented, look at what the teacher is doing in the classroom. The appraiser views teaching as serving a set of interrelated functions. Fisher and others (1980) provide one way of conceptualizing the instructional process. They consider teaching to consist of five interrelated functions:

> *diagnosis*—assessing the current knowledge, skill levels, strengths, and weaknesses of students
>
> *prescription*—deciding on appropriate goals and activities
>
> *presentation*—introducing concepts or learning tasks to students
>
> *monitoring*—ascertaining the students' knowledge or skills during or following an instructional activity
>
> *feedback*—providing the student with knowledge of results

When looking at the classroom from the vantage point of these five functions, the appraiser seeks to determine whether each of the functions is being performed by the teacher and what specific teacher behaviors are actually being used to fulfill the function. According to Fisher and his colleagues, each function can be fulfilled in a variety of ways. For example, "diagnosis may be accomplished by listening to a child read, talking to a child about what she is interested in, watching the way a student works during an independent seatwork assignment, giving formal tests, etc." By focusing on these five interrelated functions, the appraiser can gain insight into how a teacher facilitates student learning.

A fourth possible focus of classroom observation is on student responses. One type of student response that is of current interest is the student's time-on-task. The amount of time a student spends on academic learning tasks is positively, though weakly, related to achievement (Karweit 1983). An appraiser may choose to focus on the extent to which students are paying attention to the learning tasks prescribed by the teacher and are succeeding in handling these tasks. Such information can provide some indication of whether a teacher is meeting the criterion of satisfactory student progress.

Besides being able to choose a focus for their observation, appraisers also need the capacity to choose a technique for gathering their observational data. Acheson and Gall (1987) discuss and provide numerous examples of several techniques. One of these techniques is "selective verbatim." When using this technique, the supervisor makes a written record of exactly what is said in the classroom that is relevant to the focus of the observation. A second technique involves the imaginative use of classroom seating charts. The supervisor uses these seating charts to record information about the nature of the teacher's relationship to individual students in the classroom. This technique, like selective verbatim, is relatively unstructured and can be tailored to a variety of criteria for judging the effectiveness of teachers. Acheson and Gall also discuss a number of checklists and observation schedules that can be used by supervisors to gather information about what is happening in classrooms. Some of these may be relevant in their present form or need to be adapted to the district's criteria.

Ability to provide unbiased ratings. When observing and evaluating others, people typically make a number of rating errors. These errors in judgment occur in a systematic way whenever a person is cast in the role of evaluating current employees or candidates for job openings. The most common rating errors are contrast effects, first impressions, halo effects, similar-to-me effects, central tendency, and positive and negative leniency (Latham and Wexley 1981).

Contrast effects refer to the tendency of raters to evaluate a person relative to other individuals rather than on how well the person fulfills the requirements of the job. As we have implied, this type of error is especially troublesome because tenured teachers are legally entitled to be evaluated against criteria that have been adopted and publicized by the board of education. Comparisons are not necessarily illegitimate, however; they may be used as long as the criterion-relevance of the comparisons is established. By way of illustration, one principal substantiated his charges that a teacher had failed to maintain a satisfactory level of student progress by citing comparative data on how much material had been covered in various classrooms. After more than four months of school, the teacher had covered 44 pages in the English text compared with 75 to 95 pages in other classes and 93 pages in the arithmetic text compared with 158 to 160 pages by other teachers (*McLain v. Board of Education, School District, No. 52*, 183 N.E. 2d 7 [1967]). Under these circumstances, comparisons are bona fide and do not represent a type of rating error.

First impression error refers to the tendency of a supervisor to make an initially favorable or unfavorable judgment about an employee, and then ignore or distort subsequent information so as to support the initial judgment. If a supervisor were committing this error, he or she would quickly decide that a teacher was satisfactory or unsatisfactory and focus on those events in the classroom that substantiated or were consistent with his first impression.

The halo effect refers to inappropriate generalizations from one aspect of a person's performance to all aspects of a person's job performance. A halo effect is operating if a supervisor judges a teacher to be satisfactory on one criterion that he regards as important—for example, classroom discipline—and then erroneously concludes that the teacher satisfies all other criteria. Conversely, a halo effect may have a detrimental impact on the teacher if the supervisor feels that the social-emotional climate of the classroom is unsatisfactory and then rates the teacher deficient on all criteria even though these ratings are inappropriate.

The similar-to-me effect is used to describe the tendency of raters to evaluate more favorably those people whom they perceive as similar to themselves. Supervisors who rate teachers more favorably if they resemble the rater's attitudes, background, gender, or race may be guilty of the similar-to-me error. Rating errors of this nature pose special difficulties if women and minorities are involved because they are members of a protected class and are also entitled to legal protection against discrimination.

Central tendency error refers to the tendency of supervisors to rate employees close to the midpoint of a scale when their performance justifies a substantially higher or lower rating. The supervisor, in effect, chooses not to make any discrimination among teachers; they are all rated as average.

The final type of rating error is negative and positive leniency, the tendency to rate employees either too harshly or too easily. In educational settings positive leniency is the more common error. Supervisors are wont to rate all teachers as outstanding or above average (Bridges 1974). This tendency to inflate the ratings of teachers creates major problems for school administrators who are determined to dismiss incompetent teachers. Such teachers may have accumulated five, ten, or even fifteen years of satisfactory evaluations from lenient raters. This history of satisfactory performance must be overcome by a compelling record of current incompetence. Difficult as this problem may be, it is not insurmountable. A black school teacher who was deemed an adequate teacher at a black school for eight years was dismissed for incompetence following transfer to a white school pursuant to a desegregation order. The district presented a substantial case against the teacher, and a principal testified before the board and the district court that, to preserve racial harmony, he had submitted favorable evaluations that were greatly at variance with his actual opinion of the teacher's competence. The dismissal was upheld by the United States Court of Appeals, Eighth Circuit (*R. Country v. R. Parratt, No. 79-2082*, 623 F. 2d 51 [1980]).

Ability to diagnose. Having concluded that the teacher is a poor performer, the supervisor needs to pinpoint the reason or combination of reasons for the substandard performance. As we noted in our discussion of remediation, these reasons may take a variety of forms. The causes for poor performance fall into three major categories: (1) managerial and/or organizational shortcomings, (2) a shortcoming of the employee, and (3) outside or non-job-related influences. The objective of diagnosis is to determine which of these factors are responsible for the poor performance. If the teacher's failure is due to managerial or organizational shortcomings, the supervisor is not justified in recommending the teacher for dismissal.

Previous research suggests that supervisors are apt to make a fundamental error during diagnosis. Supervisors are predisposed to attribute the poor performance of subordinates to internal rather than external causes. That is to say, supervisors are inclined to attribute substandard performance to some defect in the subordinate (for example, lack of ability or effort) as opposed to some shortcomings of the organization or management. This tendency to make a fundamental error is pervasive and is strengthened if the subordinate happens to be a female or a minority (Mitchell and others 1981). Two factors appear to weaken the tendency; they are the degree of psychological closeness that exists between the supervisor and the subordinate and the extent to which the supervisor is systematic in gathering data about the causes of the poor performance.

If the supervisor commits a fundamental error when evaluating the performance of subordinates, the consequences for the poor performer depend in part on whether the supervisor makes an effort attribution or an ability attribution. *Given the same performance*, a supervisor will make more extreme evaluations if he attributes the unacceptable performance to a lack of effort (Mitchell and others 1981). Moreover, the effort attribution will lead to a more punitive response by the supervisor than will an ability attribution.

In determining whether the teacher's difficulties are due to a lack of effort or skill, the supervisor should seek answers to the following sorts of questions: Could the teacher do what is expected if his or her life depended on it? Has the teacher ever shown in the past that he or she is able to do what is expected? If the answers to both of these questions are yes, the teacher's difficulties probably reflect a lack of motivation or effort. If the answers are no, the difficulties in all likelihood are due to a lack of skill (Bridges 1985).

Ability to prescribe remediation. Although the research on staff development provides some valuable clues to supervisors for designing remediation programs, there is no conclusive evidence that these programs will produce the same kinds of results for the problem teacher. Researchers have shown little interest in studying how the needs of incompetent teachers might be addressed. As a result, supervisors will need to adopt an experimental stance when designing remediation plans. Supervisors who succeed in their first attempt to effect improvement in a problem teacher's performance are likely to be the exception rather than the rule.

Prescription is directed toward correcting or eliminating a teacher's performance inadequacies. For example, if the inept performance is due to motivational deficiencies or lack of effort, the supervisor needs to be able to pinpoint the behaviors to be changed and to identify the types of feedback that should be provided to the teacher, the types and schedules of reinforcement that should be administered, and the steps that should be taken to maintain the changes in behavior. On the other hand, if the problem of incompetence stems from a skill deficiency, the supervisor needs to be able to specify the skill-related knowledge that should be transmitted to the teacher, to create opportunities for the teacher to observe someone modeling the skill, to arrange opportunities for the teacher to practice the skill, to provide feedback on the teacher's attempts to use the skill, and to provide assistance (coaching) to the teacher as he or she seeks to incorporate this skill into her regular classroom teaching practices.

Since diagnosis and prescription are presently an inexact science, supervisors need to view their efforts as testing a hypothesis. As with all hypotheses, they may turn out to be either true or false. If the initial hypothesis proves to be false and the teacher shows little or no progress, it may be due to a faulty diagnosis, an inappropriate prescription, or both. In light of these two possibilities, supervisors should reconsider the diagnosis, as well as the prescription, and formulate and test a new hypothesis. The supervisor probably will need to test several hypotheses before a valid one emerges.

Ability to conduct conferences. Four approaches can be used in conducting appraisal interviews—Tell and Sell, Tell and Listen, Problem-Solving, and Quasi-Problem-Solving. The skill requirements for each of these types of appraisal interviews differ. Likewise, the objectives for each kind of interview are dissimilar.

In the Tell and Sell interview, the supervisor has three primary objectives: (1) to let employees know how well they are doing, (2) to gain their acceptance of the evaluation, and (3) to obtain their acceptance of a plan for improvement if deficiencies are noted. This type of interview requires skills in communicating clearly and in overcoming the resistance that may accompany negative evaluations and suggestions for change or improvement.

The Tell and Listen method has two major objectives. One of these, letting employees know where they stand, is identical to the Tell and Sell approach. The other objective is to allow the employee an opportunity to release feelings aroused by the evaluation. Adherents of the Tell and Listen method assume two roles during the appraisal—judge and counselor. The judge role occurs during the first part of the interview and requires competence in communicating information clearly and directly. The counselor role predominates in the second half of the appraisal interview and demands four kinds of skills—active listening, effective use of pauses, reflection of feelings, and summary of feelings (Maier 1976). Little emphasis is placed on developing a program for improvement since this is not an important objective of the Tell and Listen approach.

Unlike either the Tell and Listen or the Tell and Sell appraisal interviews, the Problem-Solving approach does not seek to communicate an evaluation of the employee's performance. Rather, the central objective is to uncover ways in which the subordinate's performance can be made more personally satisfying and efficient. Accordingly, the supervisor requires skills in framing exploratory questions, in summarizing key points of the discussion, and in using pauses (Maier 1976). The evaluation is downplayed and introduced near the end of the interview, if at all.

The Quasi-Problem-Solving method has three principal objectives: (l) to apprise employees of how well they are doing; (2) to determine the reasons, external as well as internal, that may account for good and poor performance; and (3) to develop a plan that is designed to remove any obstacles standing in the way of a satisfactory or outstanding performance. In accomplishing the first objective, the supervisor is the dominant actor and acts in a judgmental role. The last two objectives entail mutual exploration and problem-solving by the supervisor and the employee. Unlike the other methods, the Quasi-Problem-Solving approach seeks to understand the ingredients of satisfactory, as well as unsatisfactory, performance and to focus on ways of improving performance even if it is currently satisfactory. This particular approach requires skills in communicating clearly, in framing exploratory questions, and in fostering cooperative problem-solving.

For most employees, the Tell and Listen, Problem-Solving, and Quasi-Problem-Solving approaches are likely to be effective and appropriate. However, if the employee's performance is unsatisfactory in one or more respects, the supervisor at some point must conduct a Tell and Sell interview or use the Quasi-Problem-Solving method as these are the only approaches that fulfill two important legal requirements—let employees know how well they are doing and establish a plan for improving the performance. The reader who desires to learn more about the Tell and Sell, Tell and Listen, and Problem-Solving methods should consult Maier (1976); Lefton and others (1980) provide an extensive treatment of the Quasi-Problem-Solving approach.

Ability to document. A supervisor needs skills in developing a system of documentation that fully supports a decision to dismiss a tenured teacher for incompetence. Since the burden of proof rests on the school district, the supervisor, as well as the incompetent teacher, is on trial. If the supervisor is to be found innocent of arbitrary, capricious behavior, he or she needs to document the events related to the evaluation and dismissal of the incompetent teacher thoroughly and adequately. Without a soundly documented case, the judgment of the supervisor will be severely tested and found wanting. Although judges believe that a school district is not married to mediocrity, they are unwilling to sanction a divorce without just cause.

To develop a sound system of documentation, the supervisor requires three basic skills. The first of these skills involves the capacity to distinguish between factual and judgmental statements. Factual statements describe events as they actually happened; these descriptions are free of conclusions, interpretations, and opinions. Judgmental statements, on the other hand, express opinions about the worth or value of an event or set of events. For example, a supervisor might prepare the following factual statements:

1. From September 15 to December 15 you referred 37 students to the office for disciplinary action.
2. On October 16 during your lecture on earthquakes, four students were drawing pictures and six children were out of their seats.
3. On December 7 nine children were sitting on their desks and four students were shouting to each other across the room while you were giving a homework assignment.

Based on numerous factual statements of this sort, the supervisor might then prepare a judgmental statement such as, "You are unable to maintain a satisfactory level of discipline in your classroom." A sound system of documentation includes judgmental statements that are supported by a number of relevant factual statements.

The second skill is closely related to the first one and involves the capacity to prepare written records that establish a pattern of poor performance in relation to the district criteria for evaluating teachers. Because there are no clearcut standards or yardsticks for determining whether a teacher is meeting a particular criterion, a supervisor must accumulate numerous examples of the teacher's shortcomings and use these instances to demonstrate that a pattern exists. The significance of a demonstrable pattern is underscored in the following statement by a judge in the Appellate Court of Illinois, Third District:

> Proof of momentary lapses in discipline or of a single day's lesson gone awry is not sufficient to show cause for dismissal of a tenured teacher.... Yet, where brief instances and isolated lapses occur repeatedly, there emerges a pattern of behavior which, if deficient, will support the dismissal of a tenured teacher. Where the school board fails . . . to show that the examples of conduct constitute a pattern of deficiency, then dismissal cannot be permitted. (*Board of Education v. Ingels*, 394 N. E. 2d 69 [1979])

A third skill needed by a supervisor is the capacity to prepare written records that cannot be refuted by an adversarial third party and that are persuasive to superiors and independent third parties such as judges or arbitrators. Since documentation plays a pivotal role in dismissal proceedings, the attorney of the dismissed teacher will seek to undermine the credibility of the written record. Superiors will need to be convinced that a sufficiently strong case exists to warrant the expenditure of district money and time. In addition to demonstrating that a written record of recurring deficiencies exists, the supervisor needs written proof to verify that:

1. the teacher received copies of the relevant documentation
2. the documentation was delivered in a timely manner
3. the teacher was given an opportunity to refute or comment on what the supervisor had written
4. the supervisor was impartial
5. the persons who filed written complaints will later testify to their authenticity

These matters, along with numerous examples and helpful guidelines for school administrators, are discussed in Frels and Cooper (1986), Carey (1981), and Moore (1980).

Knowledge of the legal aspects. Teacher evaluation and dismissal are filled with a plethora of legal pitfalls and requirements. When a supervisor first suspects that a tenured teacher may need to be dismissed for incompetence, the supervisor should seek expert guidance and counsel from an attorney. Although the supervisor should rely heavily on legal counsel in navigating the legal minefield during this difficult period, the supervisor also needs a working knowledge of the legal basis for teacher evaluation and dismissal so as to use an attorney effectively.

Teacher evaluation and dismissal decisions are governed primarily by state statutes, school board rules and regulations, local collective bargaining agreements, and the United States Constitution. State statutes generally provide the greatest number of elements in the legal structure, and the supervisor needs to know what the provisions of these statutes are in his state. Specifically, the supervisor must have knowledge of the statutory provisions related to: criteria, methods of evaluation, access to personnel records, notices, remedial assistance, hearings, appeals, remedies for wrongful discharge, and the timelines or deadlines associated with these matters.

In addition, the supervisor needs to know if the board of education has adopted any rules or regulations relating to teacher evaluation and dismissal or has entered into a collective bargaining agreement that contains provisions pertinent to the evaluation and dismissal of teachers. These rules, regulations, and contractual agreements must be strictly adhered to by the supervisor. Finally, the supervisor needs to understand the meaning of substantive and procedural due process because the Fourteenth Amendment guarantees these rights to tenured teachers. A comprehensive discussion of these various aspects appears in Beckham (1985).

COMPETENCY ASSURANCE PROGRAMS

As we mentioned at the outset of this discussion on supervisor knowledge and skills, a school district cannot assume that its administrative personnel possess these essential competencies and understandings. The superintendent must implement ways of ensuring that its current and prospective supervisors have the knowledge and skills required to perform their evaluative responsibilities effectively. There are at least three alternatives for the superintendent to consider: (l) selection, (2) inservice education, and (3) printed materials.

Selection. When considering applicants for administrative positions within the district, selection committees can be instructed to gather information relative to each of the competencies that we have discussed. Experienced candidates may be asked to submit samples of their evaluations, observation reports, and conference memos. Finalists may be required to view a videotape or a film of a classroom teaching episode, to provide a written analysis of what was observed, and to role-play a conference with a teacher. Finalists also may be questioned during the interview about how they intend to detect and to deal with incompetent teachers. These possibilities are not mutually exclusive and may all be used during the selection process.

Inservice education. Since a school district's current stable of supervisors may lack one or more of the requisite competencies, the superintendent may wish to use these as the focus of an inservice education program for principals and other instructional supervisors. The Lake Washington School District near Seattle has developed an elaborate program to teach principals skills in analyzing instruction, note taking, and conducting conferences (McLaughlin 1984). This particular program relies heavily on videotapes and printed materials produced and distributed by Madeline Hunter. Since the approach adopted by Lake Washington is quite expensive, most districts probably will be unable to afford a program of this type unless they are willing to form a regional cooperative.

Printed materials. School districts also may foster competent supervisory performance by preparing printed materials and manuals.

These materials may explain the concept of due process and spell out what principals must do to ensure due process for teachers during the evaluation process. Additionally, these materials may offer a timetable and a step-by-step checklist of the procedures that are mandated by state statutes and the collective bargaining contract. Finally, these materials may contain guidelines for preparing documentation, samples of competent documentation and assistance or remediation plans, and definitions of key terms. If a district has such materials available, they can be used to provide inservice training for principals and to orient new school board members to what is involved in evaluating and dismissing teachers. (For an excellent example of such materials see Tolleson 1989.)

6

Provide the Necessary Resources

If supervisors are to fulfill their responsibilities for evaluating the instructional staff, they need a variety of resources. Specifically, supervisors need time, authority, access to remedial assistance, access to legal counsel, and support. Without these particular resources supervisors are unlikely to meet the organization's role expectations even if they are committed to performing the appraisal function effectively and have the requisite skills and knowledge. Supervisory effort and ability are necessary but insufficient conditions for effective performance appraisal; organizational resources also play a crucial role in the process of evaluating and dismissing incompetent teachers.

TIME

According to Mackenzie (1972), time is an organization's scarcest and most critical resource. Moreover, of all organizational resources time is the least understood and most mismanaged (Mackenzie). Unless superintendents consciously address the issue of time and take steps to deal with it, the scarcity of this important resource is apt to cripple any concerted attempt to evaluate, improve, and dismiss teachers who are incompetent classroom performers.

Time is an especially acute problem for the principal, the person who commonly bears major responsibility for evaluating teachers. The appraisal function is but one of the many functions performed by principals. They also have functional responsibilities in matters relating to student discipline, school-community relations, curriculum development, and school facilities. The one area that consistently suffers from neglect is the supervision of instruction (Hallinger 1983).

To ensure that sufficient time is available for evaluating and dismissing teachers who do not respond to remediation, the superintendent needs to adopt policies and practices that focus directly on this critical problem. One way is to establish priorities among the functions and tasks contained in job descriptions for the role of principal. Given the multiple responsibilities of principals, top management needs to establish a hierarchy of importance among these myriad functions. This hierarchy prescribes the trade-offs that inevitably must be made in fulfilling any organizational role and discourages principals from sacrificing objectives that are cherished by the institution.

Another way superintendents can ensure that time is available for dealing with problem classroom teachers is to institute time conservation measures. The dismissal of a tenured teacher and the procedures that accompany this admittedly distasteful task are time consuming. School districts can provide this time by limiting the amount of time their principals are required to spend on teachers who have a history of satisfactory or outstanding performance in the classroom. For such teachers, other types of supervisory personnel (for example, department heads, assistant principals, and supervisors of elementary or secondary education) might be used while the principal is working intensively with one or more teachers who are "at risk" of losing their positions.

AUTHORITY

Studies conducted in the late 1960s and early 1970s reveal that collective bargaining agreements may erode the supervisory authority of principals and, thereby, impede their ability to perform their supervisory responsibilities effectively (Educational Research Service 1979). One type of authority that is particularly vulnerable to negotiations involves the inspection rights of principals. Teacher organizations attempt to limit the frequency of classroom observations and to prohibit them from being unannounced. If supervisors lack the authority to decide how many observations are warranted for a given teacher, they in all likelihood will be unable to establish that a pattern of performance deficiencies exists. Moreover, if all observations must be announced in advance, the supervisor may never even see a representative sample of the teacher's poor performance because he or she has staged the lesson. For these reasons, the superintendent needs to protect the inspection rights of principals or to restore these rights if the collective bargaining agreement curtails them.

In addition to inspection rights, principals and supervisors need the authority to use a variety of sources and types of information in evaluating teachers. More precisely, supervisors should possess the right to use student ratings, student progress, parent complaints, and student complaints, along with classroom observations, to establish the incompetence of a teacher. Although the courts attach great weight to supervisory evaluations based on classroom observations, principals can strengthen their cases against incompetent teachers by drawing upon different types of evidence to substantiate their claims.

Finally, supervisors who are obligated to prescribe a program of remediation for an incompetent teacher should have the organizationally sanctioned right to expect and, if necessary, to demand the compliance of the teacher with this plan of assistance. If the teacher refuses to comply, this refusal should be considered insubordination and constitute cause for dismissal. Unless the obligations of the supervisor and the subordinate are explicitly reciprocal, the supervisor also faces the difficult and unpleasant task of persuading the teacher of the merits of the improvement plan.

ACCESS TO REMEDIAL ASSISTANCE

Since the supervisor's competence in prescribing remedial assistance is apt to be weak and his or her ability to provide this assistance is likely to be hampered by a lack of time and subject matter expertise, the supervisor needs easy access to remedial assistance. The district can supply this assistance through a variety of mechanisms—self-instructional materials, inservice education, mentors, and money. At this juncture, nothing is known about the relative effectiveness of these various mechanisms.

Self-instructional materials that are targeted toward commonly occurring teaching deficiencies represent a potentially inexpensive means for providing some of this remedial assistance. These self-instructional materials may be in written form and consist of books, booklets, or articles that focus on particular problems like discipline or lesson planning. Or these materials may be presented through audiovisual media such as films or videotapes. Ideally, these instructional materials should provide the teacher with knowledge relevant to the teacher's deficiencies, concrete examples of teachers using this knowledge in a skillful manner, practice in applying this information, and feedback to the teacher about his or her mastery of the relevant skills and knowledge. Luehe and Ehrgott (1981) have written a book that incorporates all four of these learning features in connection with planning and implementing an effective lesson.

If the school district has designed its inservice education program with remediation as a primary objective, supervisors may be able to use this mechanism to assist teachers. Because such programs are usually planned a year in advance, school districts can survey supervisors to determine the specific problems that teachers are currently facing. Those deficiencies for which the district lacks self-instructional materials may serve as the foci for the inservice education program. Since the timing of these various remedial programs may affect their value to the teacher and the principal, supervisors should be involved in scheduling these programs.

A third type of remedial assistance that may be made available to supervisors who are working with problem teachers is the mentor or master teacher. Salt Lake City, by way of illustration, uses assisting teachers in its formal remediation program (Wise and others 1984). These teachers spend a period of time, from a week to a month based on individual need, with the teacher on remediation. According to the collective bargaining agreement, these assisting teachers shall be drawn from among retired teachers or teachers on leave. The Lake Washington School District employs five full-time trainers to work with teachers in need of assistance (McLaughlin 1984). These trainers are thoroughly familiar with the materials and techniques of Madeline Hunter and use these in their staff development activities. Unlike the situation that prevails in Salt Lake City, the trainers in Lake Washington are prohibited by contract from discussing the teacher's problems with an administrator and testifying against the teacher in a dismissal proceeding.

Lastly, a school district may allocate money to principals for remedial purposes. These discretionary funds can be used to hire substitutes, either for the problem teacher who is freed to visit the classrooms of outstanding teachers or for mentors who are freed to work with the problem teacher. These funds might also be used to employ consultants who have expertise in dealing with particular problems. Alternatively, this money might enable the teacher who is in difficulty to attend a workshop or a course offered by a local university, to obtain counseling assistance, or to offset some of the costs associated with participating in a therapeutic program.

ACCESS TO LEGAL COUNSEL

Even if supervisors believe that they are familiar with the Constitutional and statutory provisions relating to the evaluation and dismissal of the incompetent teacher, they should be encouraged to consult with competent legal counsel who is in a position to devote the necessary time and attention to the problem at hand. Ideally, this attorney should be a specialist in teacher dismissals; otherwise, he or she may be unable to fulfill the needs of the supervisor. Worse yet, the advice may be ill-founded and inadvertently contribute to losing the case against the teacher.

SUPPORT

Supervisors may pay a high psychological price for their involvement in the evaluation and dismissal of incompetent teachers. Both of these activities may arouse such powerful emotions as fear, self-doubt, anger, and guilt. Fear or feelings of danger may arise because the supervisor suspects that other teachers will resent his or her actions and retaliate by flooding him with grievances or by undertaking a hidden campaign to discredit him in the eyes of the community. Feelings of self-doubt may be engendered if the supervisor senses that he or she lacks one or more of the skills needed to build a defensible case against the incompetent teacher. Anger may be aroused because the supervisor is frustrated by the need to spend so much time and energy on an unrewarding task. Guilt may arise when the supervisor recognizes that dismissal will deprive the teacher and his or her family of their livelihood. All these negative emotions are ever-present possibilities that may deter the supervisor from fulfilling his organizational obligations or may threaten his physical and mental well-being if he chooses to proceed.

The superintendent needs to anticipate these emotional reactions and to provide the supervisor with the backing and the emotional support required during this potentially difficult period. Specifically, the chief executive needs to supply verbal *and* written assurance that the supervisor's actions are authorized by the superintendent and that the recommendation to dismiss will be backed fully by the superintendent. In addition, the superintendent needs to encourage supervisors to talk about what is happening and their reactions to these events. If the superintendent expresses concern for and understanding of what supervisors are experiencing during this process, they are more likely to cope successfully with the stress that accompanies these emotionally demanding situations and to carry out their responsibilities for evaluating and dismissing unsatisfactory employees.

7

Hold Supervisors Accountable

Principals are primarily responsible for teacher evaluation (Educational Research Service 1979, Groves 1985), and they express the belief that they should spend a large portion of their time in classrooms working with teachers (Carey 1981). However, the available research indicates that principals do not allocate a significant portion of their time to managing instructional activities (Hallinger 1983). They perform infrequent evaluations of instruction, and these are often ritualistic occasions for "ceremonial congratulations" (Guthrie and Willower 1973). In place of coordinating and controlling the technology of education (that is, curriculum and instruction), principals spend most of their workday on managerial tasks that are unrelated to instructional technology (Peterson 1977-78, Sproull 1981).

To disrupt this oft-observed pattern of administrator behavior, a school district needs to hold principals accountable for spending more time on instructional matters and for dealing forthrightly with unsatisfactory teachers. Specifically, a district should adopt and enforce policies that (1) discourage supervisors from inflating the evaluations of incompetent teachers; (2) counter the tendencies of supervisors to postpone dealing with an incompetent teacher and to use rationalizations that bolster their procrastination; (3) discourage supervisors from passing the poor performer to someone else in the district; and (4) encourage principals to provide instructional leadership.

INFLATED RATINGS

Inflated performance ratings are common to all types of organizations (Mitchell and others 1981), and elementary and secondary educational institutions are no exception (Bridges 1990). Few teachers receive average or unsatisfactory ratings; even fewer are dismissed. Unsatisfactory ratings generate time demands, expenditure of effort, and unpleasantness for the supervisor, while satisfactory or outstanding ratings, if unchallenged, are accompanied by positive feelings and outcomes. The field of positive and negative reinforcements generally favor positive leniency by supervisors as we pointed out earlier.

To counter this type of rating error, school districts have several options. They may adopt the "Review of Services" procedure used by Salt Lake City, or they may institute exit interviews with parents leaving the district to ascertain, among other things, whom they judge to be particularly outstanding or poor teachers. If principals do inflate the ratings, they can be reprimanded, denied salary increments, or placed on probation.

PROCRASTINATION AND RATIONALIZATION

If a principal realizes that one of her teachers is incompetent, she may be in conflict about what to do. The principal experiences conflict because she believes something should be done; however, she recognizes that there is no easy resolution to the problem. If the principal loses hope of finding a satisfactory solution and foresees no serious risks if she postpones action, the principal is likely to procrastinate and to use rationalizations that bolster her inaction (Janis and Mann 1977). Some common rationalizations or excuses are as follows:

1. "It's too costly."
2. "You can never win."
3. "It's too time consuming."
4. "The morale of my staff would be destroyed."
5. "The next teacher will be even worse."

To counter these rationalizations, districts may use a procedure developed by Janis and Mann (1977). The object of this procedure is to make individuals aware of their rationalizations and to present information designed to refute each of their rationalizations. The procedure begins by asking questions like the following:

> "Have you ever said this to excuse your reluctance to deal with an incompetent teacher?"
>
> "Has this excuse ever occurred to you?"
>
> "Do you think that, deep down, this might be a reasonable or valid argument?"
>
> "Have you ever heard another principal use this excuse?"

For each excuse or rationalization, information is presented to counteract it; for example, let us consider how the "It's too costly" excuse might be refuted:

> "Yes, dismissal is a costly process. The exact costs are unknown at this point, however. Estimates on the higher end of the scale

range from fifty to one hundred thousand dollars. All of these estimates make the no-benefit assumption; that is to say, they are based on the assumption that the district receives no financial benefits from the dismissal. This no-benefit assumption is erroneous. If an experienced teacher is replaced with a beginning teacher, there is an annual savings produced by the difference between the salaries of the two teachers. The more experienced the teacher, the greater is the savings. When these savings are taken into account, the district is apt to recover its costs in three to five years and experience an actual decline in employee costs after the break-even point has been reached. Besides, financial costs and benefits are not the determining factor in this district anyway. Teacher effectiveness is far more important than costs!"

To take another example, the "You can never win" excuse might be countered as follows:

"Difficult yes; impossible, no. As districts become more sophisticated in assembling their cases against incompetent teachers, school officials are winning dismissal cases when they are contested by teachers. Between 1977 and 1987, 90 percent of the cases charging teachers with incompetence and inefficiency in the state of New York were settled in favor of the district. In other states hearing panels, hearing officers, and court judges are also sustaining the dismissal decisions of school districts. Our district has employed expert legal counsel to assist you in preparing a case that has a high probability of being upheld. So, never say never again!"

Finally, the "It's too time consuming" rationalization might be refuted in the following way:

"There is no question that working with incompetent teachers takes a lot of time. If you make a concerted effort to assist a teacher who is having difficulty, you will probably spend up to ten hours per week over a period of three or four months observing this person in the classroom, holding conferences with him or her to discuss your observations and suggestions for improvement, and documenting what has taken place. If you have more than one problem teacher under your supervision, you should select the worst performer and concentrate your efforts on that person. No one expects you to solve every personnel problem in a single year. To make the situation manageable, work on one problem at a time and let us know what your overall strategy is. If you need relief or assistance along the way, ask for it and we'll try to help you out."

BUCK-PASSING

Passing-the-buck is an all-time favorite game in organizations. When faced with difficult decisions for which there are no completely satisfactory solutions, people have a tendency to shift the responsibility for dealing with these situations to someone else within the organization. In school circles the practice of moving incompetent teachers from one school principal to another is referred to as "the dance of the lemons" or "pass the turkey" (Bridges 1990, Brieschke 1986). To counter the "turkey trot," some districts have adopted unique transfer policies like the following: if a teacher receives a positive evaluation in one school, transfers to another, and then encounters difficulty in the new setting, the teacher is returned to the first school and *the principal* is placed under surveillance (Downey 1978).

INSTRUCTIONAL LEADERSHIP

In addition to these specific measures for dealing with principals who are reluctant to perform their roles as supervisors of instruction, the school district may stimulate interest in instructional management through its ongoing evaluation of principals. If a district assigns great weight to instructional leadership in its principal appraisal program and links salary increases to performance in this area, principals will be more inclined to emphasize this hitherto neglected responsibility.

The Instructional Management Rating Scales developed by Hallinger (1983) offer a promising approach to evaluating principals in their role as instructional managers. He has constructed eleven scales based on the school effectiveness research; these rating scales are sound and possess satisfactory reliability and validity for evaluating elementary principals. Several of these scales and sample items are reproduced on the following pages.

These scales are especially valuable because they can be used by local school districts to clarify the meaning of instructional leadership, a heretofore nebulous concept. Moreover, the behaviors contained in these scales are behaviors that previous research has found to be characteristic of effective schools, that is, schools where students perform better than expected given their ability and socioeconomic background.

Scale III. Supervision and Evaluation of Instruction

	Almost Never				Almost Always	
13. Conducts informal observations in classrooms on a regular basis.	1	2	3	4	5	?
14. Ensures that the classroom objectives of						

teachers are consistent with the stated goals
of the school.   1   2   3   4   5   ?

16. Reviews student work products when
evaluating teachers.   1   2   3   4   5   ?

19. Points out specific weaknesses of the teacher's instructional practices in post-observation conferences.   1   2   3   4   5   ?

22. Notes student time on task in feedback to teachers after classroom observations.   1   2   3   4   5   ?

Scale V. Monitoring and Feeding Back Student Performance Results

31. Meets individually with teachers to discuss pupil academic performance.   1   2   3   4   5   ?

32. Discusses the item analysis of districtwide tests with the faculty in order to identify strengths and weaknesses in the school's instructional program.   1   2   3   4   5   ?

34. Distributes the results of student testing to teachers in a timely fashion.   1   2   3   4   5   ?

Scale VIII. Promoting Incentives to Improve Teaching

49. Reinforces superior performance by teachers publicly in newsletters or bulletins.   1   2   3   4   5   ?

50. Privately recognizes teacher efforts and performance.   1   2   3   4   5   ?

Scale IX. Promoting Instructional Improvement and Professional Development

56. Distributes journal articles to teachers on a regular basis.   1   2   3   4   5   ?

60. Provides time to meet individually with teachers to discuss instructional issues.   1   2   3   4   5   ?

62. Sets aside time at faculty meetings for teachers to share information concerning their classroom experiences and in-service activities.   1   2   3   4   5   ?

8

Provide Fair Hearing Prior to Dismissal

A tenured teacher has a "property" interest in his or her position under the Fourteenth Amendment; therefore, school districts must provide the teacher with a fair hearing prior to depriving the teacher of his position.

COMPONENTS OF A FAIR HEARING

Generally, the necessary components of a fair hearing are delineated in state statutes. These statutes may entitle the teacher to some or all of the following rights:

1. a statement of charges and the materials upon which they are based
2. a hearing before the school board, a hearing panel, or a hearing officer if requested
3. a timely written notice of the date, time, and place of the hearing
4. a hearing in public or private
5. an opportunity to be represented by counsel
6. an opportunity to call witnesses on his own behalf
7. an opportunity to subpoena a person who has made allegations that are used as a basis for the decision of the employer
8. an opportunity to cross-examine witnesses
9. witness testimony under oath or affirmation
10. a shorthand reporting or tape recording of the hearing upon request
11. a written decision that contains the specific findings or grounds on which it is based
12. a written statement of his or her rights to appeal

If the district fails to provide the teacher with any of the hearing rights mandated by state statutes, the dismissal decision may be set aside. Therefore, the district must consult legal counsel to ensure that it will strictly observe the teacher's procedural rights. A comprehensive discussion of the legal issues that can arise in public school administrative hearings appears in Phay (1982).

During an administrative hearing, there are three major participants—adjudicator, district administration, and teacher. The adjudicator listens to the evidence and the arguments of the district administration and the teacher, weighs the importance of what has been presented by both sides, and renders a decision or proposed decision. The district administration attempts to establish the incompetence of the teacher and often relies on the principal, the superintendent, the school attorney, and other witnesses such as students or parents to accomplish this task. Those individuals who are on the side of the teacher attempt to defend the teacher against the accusations of the district administration; these people usually are the teacher himself, his legal counsel, and fellow teachers.

If the board of education is the adjudicator, it is highly important for the board to maintain as much distance from the district administration as possible during the dismissal proceeding. Otherwise, the board risks voiding the entire procedure because it subjects itself to the legal argument that it has not provided the teacher with a fair hearing. For example, during the hearing, legal issues, such as the admissibility of a particular piece or type of evidence, may arise on which the board must rule. Should the board turn to advice from the school attorney who is advising the school administration, it may violate the teacher's right to a fair hearing.

Alternatively, the board may be tempted to seek advice from the superintendent or invite the superintendent to be present during its deliberations. If the superintendent has brought charges against the teacher or testified on behalf of the district administration, the board jeopardizes the validity of the hearing. Under these circumstances, the mere presence of the superintendent during the board's deliberations constitutes a potentially fatal legal flaw (Phay 1982). These examples underscore the need of the board to maintain its independence from the district administration in relation to the teacher's hearing.

PHASES OF DISMISSAL PROCEEDINGS

Dismissal proceedings may go through a number of phases. Some of the most common phases include discovery, direct examination, cross-examination, closing argument, and deliberation. Let us examine each of these phases and consider some of the problems and legal issues that may arise.

Discovery. Prior to the hearing, the opposing parties may disclose information and evidence that they propose to use in the hearing. This disclosure prevents the type of "trial by ambush" that is so familiar to Perry Mason fans. Discovery is designed to avoid surprises and to expedite the proceedings; it is usually mandated by state statute. During the discovery phase, the district administration is generally obligated to provide all information regarding the dates and times of incidents relevant to each charge, the names and addresses of potential witnesses, and copies of any affidavits or exhibits that may be introduced at the hearing.

Direct examination. This is usually the first phase of the actual hearing. During this phase, the district administration seeks to establish that a pattern of incompetent performance exists despite efforts to assist the teacher in overcoming these deficiencies. The principal's testimony and documentation play an important role in this phase; in fact, they often represent the most significant element of the district's presentation. While conducting the direct examination, the attorney for the district administration cannot ask the principal leading questions, questions that suggest the desired answer. An example of such a question is as follows:

> "Did the teacher's failure to meet deadlines and his refusal to accept committee assignments demonstrate inadequate service to the school community and a lack of potential for being a good teacher?" This question is leading. It really states a conclusion and makes clear that the questioner wants the witness to answer, "Yes." (Phay 1982)

Since the attorney cannot assist the principal by asking leading questions, the principal must be thoroughly familiar with the evidence and the testimony that need to be presented in support of each charge. However, the principal is not solely dependent on his or her memory and ability to recall; she may refer to notes and documentation that she has prepared in connection with the teacher's dismissal.

Cross-examination. This aspect of a hearing is perhaps the most emotionally demanding one for the school administration. In this phase, the attorney for the teacher seeks to discredit the administration by asking questions that are designed to establish one or more of the following (taken in large part from Evans n.d.):

1. That the administration failed to comply with established state law(s) and/or local board policies and related rules and regulations. For example, the principal failed to provide the teacher with a sufficiently specific statement of deficiencies.
2. That the administration practiced "unequal application of the law." That is to say, the teacher was criticized for acts for which other teachers, acting in a similar manner, received no such criticism.
3. That the administration was biased against the teacher. The

defense counsel will try to establish that "philosophical" differences, not deficiencies in teaching skills, accounted for the teacher's difficulties, or the teacher has become a target of the administration because of his activities in the union.

4. That the administration did not give adequate support and guidance to the teacher. In other words, supervisor shortcomings account for the teacher's failure to improve his performance.
5. That the administration "harassed" the teacher through holding an excessive number of classroom observations and conferences. As a result, the teacher became overanxious and was unable to improve.
6. That the administration was remiss in not explicitly proscribing certain behavior for the teacher. For example, the principal stated, "It would be helpful if . . ." and "I would appreciate it if . . . ." Such statements, according to the defendant's legal counsel, do not let the teacher know that the behavior is unacceptable and should be stopped.
7. That the administration cannot prove that alleged written or oral communication with the teacher actually occurred. "You never told me."
8. That the administration "influenced" the original perception of witnesses and/or their subsequent testimony.
9. That the credibility of administrative testimony is suspect with respect to lack of subject matter expertise, relevant teaching experience at the teacher's grade level and administrative experience in supervising and evaluating teachers.
10. That the administrator's recollections of specific details are hazy and subject to confusion.

In preparing for the cross-examination phase, school administrators in consultation with their attorney should carefully consider these potential lines of attack by the defense and develop appropriate and effective responses.

Closing argument. When both sides have completed the presentation of their evidence, the attorneys for the school district and the teacher make their final oral argument to the adjudicator. Since the burden of proof rests on the school district, the school attorney has the opportunity to speak first and last. At the conclusion of the closing arguments, the adjudicator recesses the hearing for the purpose of deliberation.

Deliberation. During the deliberation phase, the adjudicator reviews the evidence to determine whether there is just cause (in this instance, cause is incompetence) for the proposed dismissal action and whether any of the teacher's substantive and procedural rights have been violated. If the adjudicator is the board of education, the members of the board should carry on their deliberations without the assistance of the superintendent, the school attorney, or anyone else who has been involved in presenting the case against the teacher (Phay 1982).

In deciding whether there is cause for dismissal, the adjudicator ordinarily considers three interrelated issues (Thurston forthcoming). The first of these relates to whether there is factual support for the claims made by the district that the teacher is incompetent. At the heart of this issue is the credibility of the witnesses and the overall evidence to support the alleged incompetence. Although dismissal cases often rest on testimony from administrators, students, and parents, the observations and evaluations of principals and assistant principals appear to be the most persuasive when they are regularly kept in a systematic way.

A second issue that figures prominently in deciding whether there is cause for dismissal revolves around the question of whether the evidence, even if it is true, is sufficient to warrant dismissal. Isolated and unrelated instances of improper behavior are generally insufficient unless they are patently outrageous (for example, using extreme racist, sexist, or sexually evocative material and grading student work without ever reading it). In determining whether the evidence is sufficient, adjudicators commonly look for evidence that a pattern exists as reflected in the repeated occurrence of the same deficiencies (for example, problems of classroom management and control) over an extended period.

The final issue to be considered by the adjudicator relates to the defenses offered by the teacher. As we noted earlier, teachers may raise a variety of defenses. Some common ones include an educational philosophy different from the administration, bad teaching conditions making it impossible to teach successfully, and bias against the teacher in a variety of forms. The effectiveness of these defenses depends in part on such factors as the teacher's ability to demonstrate success with students, the strength of the district's case, and the evidence offered by the teacher to substantiate his or her various defenses.

When determining whether the evidence with respect to these three interrelated issues constitutes cause for dismissal, adjudicators commonly use preponderance of the evidence as the standard of proof. This standard of proof is less exacting than the standard used in criminal proceedings—proof beyond a reasonable doubt. *Preponderance of the evidence* is a term without precise meaning despite its frequency of use as a standard and numerous efforts to define it. The ambiguity of the term is revealed in the following excerpt from Phay (1982):

> The courts have often defined the term "preponderance of the evidence," since it is the general standard used in civil cases. The phrase probably is most easily understood as meaning a majority of the evidence, or 51 percent. It has also been defined as the greater weight of the evidence that is credible and convincing and "best accords with reason and probability. " To prove by a preponderance of the evidence means, the Connecticut Supreme Court said in a teacher dismissal case, that "the evidence must when considered fairly and impartially, induce a reasonable belief that the fact in issue is true."

Phay goes on to explain that a preponderance is not determined by the number of witnesses or exhibits but by the greater weight of all the evidence.

> The testimony of one witness may be more persuasive than that of ten, because opportunity for knowledge, information possessed, and manner of testifying determine the weight to be given to the testimony. Thus the board needs to consider only the evidence that it considers to be fair and reliable in deciding what is the preponderance of the evidence.

After reviewing the evidence presented by both sides, the adjudicator issues its ruling in writing. This written report must contain findings of fact on which the decision is based. In some states, such as North Carolina, boards that act as adjudicators are also required to include conclusions of law in their ruling. Given the legal importance of the ruling, the board should rely on the assistance of an attorney in preparing this document. This attorney, as we have underscored, should not be one who has been involved in presenting the case against the teacher.

In concluding our discussion of the hearing, we want to underscore the importance of having competent legal counsel available to prepare school administrators for this legal proceeding.

> The attorney should explain, orally and in writing, the entire dismissal proceeding and the role of the administrator in that proceeding. The attorney should also provide a realistic analysis of the strengths and weaknesses of the case and advise the client, at each step of the proceedings, of the potential pitfalls. The attorney should also exhaustively prepare an administrator for his direct testimony by preparing the questions he will be asked and by requiring the administrator to answer those questions in a situation simulating the hearing itself. Moreover, the attorney should anticipate cross-examination and prepare the client thoroughly in that regard. (Seely 1983)

9

Putting Theory into Practice

Adopting the comprehensive, integrated approach to teacher evaluation that we have described in this monograph represents a significant organizational change. Undertaking major organizational changes is rarely straightforward (McLaughlin and Pfeifer 1988). Such changes oftentimes take longer than the initiators imagine and are frequently accompanied by unanticipated problems and obstacles. To increase the likelihood of a successful adoption, the superintendent needs to create the organizational conditions that are conducive to success. These conditions include, but are not necessarily limited to, the following: situational appraisal, legitimization, teacher involvement, full accounting, and continual commitment.

SITUATIONAL APPRAISAL

A reasonable starting point for introducing the comprehensive, integrated approach to teacher evaluation that we recommend is *situational appraisal*. The purpose of situational appraisal is to determine how current district practices in the area of teacher evaluation correspond to the ones endorsed in this monograph. The District Evaluation Practices Inventory (DEPI) that appears in the Appendix can be used to conduct this appraisal and to pinpoint the needs for change.

The results of this situational appraisal will undoubtedly reveal significant discrepancies between the recommended and the actual approach to teacher evaluation. Groves (1985) found that none of the 100 school districts he studied used all eight of the recommended practices; most used two or fewer. District approaches to teacher evaluation commonly failed to offer suitable remediation programs, to hold supervisors accountable, to use satisfactory procedures for determining whether teachers met the district evaluation criteria, and to ensure that supervisors had the necessary skills to conduct teacher evaluations (Groves 1985).

LEGITIMIZATION

When introducing this comprehensive approach to teacher evaluation into a school district, it is important to legitimize the change by making it a component of a broader effort to bring about program improvement (McLaughlin and Pfeifer 1988). All the exemplary teacher evaluation programs studied by McLaughlin and Pfeifer were initiated in this way. The Charlotte-Mecklenburg, North Carolina, School District, for example, implemented its strong teacher evaluation system as a component of its innovative Career Development Program. Teachers in this district accepted the increased emphasis on evaluation when they recognized it was part of an overall program of improvement to address two interrelated problems: (1) the shortage of qualified teachers and (2) the need to raise teacher salaries.

The importance of the legitimacy issue cannot be overemphasized. Most employees, including teachers, suffer from "valuphobia" and are likely to resist an increased emphasis on evaluation unless it is embedded in a larger program of improvement that has a clear, positive, and central purpose. Those districts that treat teacher evaluation as a stand-alone concept are apt to encounter substantial opposition and resentment from their teachers (McLaughlin and Pfeifer 1988). If these negative reactions occur, the success of the effort to implement a strong teacher evaluation program is in jeopardy.

TEACHER INVOLVEMENT

If a district wants its teaching staff to support a stronger approach to teacher evaluation than ordinarily prevails in school districts, teachers should be involved during the developmental phase (McLaughlin and Pfeifer 1988). They have a stake in the outcome and possess expertise that can inform many of the decisions that lie at the heart of the organizational approach. Those decisions that seem most appropriate for teacher involvement are (1) the criteria for evaluating teachers, (2) the types of evidence to be used in determining whether teachers satisfy the criteria, and (3) the types of assistance to be afforded teachers in their quest for improved classroom performance.

Teacher involvement needs to be meaningful if it is to secure commitment to a more stringent approach to evaluation. Forming a committee of teachers and administrators to consider changes in district evaluation practices falls short of the kind of involvement that is necessary. According to the research conducted by McLaughlin and Pfeifer (1988), all teachers in the district, not just union representatives or volunteers, must be given an opportunity to participate. Broad-based teacher involvement can be promoted through a variety of means—a central steering committee composed of representatives from the teacher association, the administration, and the board; school-elected liaison teachers who channel information to and from the steering committee; anonymous suggestion and question boxes placed at every school; and periodic meetings of the steering committee chair with the faculty at each school site. The importance of this kind of meaningful involvement is reflected in the comment by a teacher association representative in the Charlotte-Mecklenburg school district:

> The answer [to why new evaluation practices seem to be working in Charlotte] is teacher input. We were involved all the way. It is true that mistakes have been made . . . and there is a need to be flexible, but the bottom line is that when teachers are being heard, success is possible. (McLaughlin and Pfeifer 1988)

FULL ACCOUNTING

In the laudable quest to improve and, failing that, to get rid of their poorly performing teachers, districts may be tempted to concentrate their limited fiscal and human resources on "at-risk" teachers. Although understandable, this decision is shortsighted and likely to be self-defeating. Teachers apparently are more receptive to evaluation when it is designed to be more than an inspection system for dealing with minimal performance (McLaughlin and Pfeifer 1988).

If evaluation is to be construed as constructive in concept, districts must be prepared to render an account for all performers—the strong as well as the weak. Teachers will view a system that is primarily driven by a concern for eliminating mediocre performance as punitive. They will be much more positive about evaluation that acknowledges exceptional, as well as poor, performance. The ability of a teacher evaluation system to achieve accountability goals in a minimalist sense seems to depend on the extent to which good performance is also recognized and good performers are challenged to become even better (McLaughlin and Pfeifer 1988). In other words, a system of teacher evaluation that is designed primarily to give only failing grades is one that is likely to fail!

CONTINUAL COMMITMENT

To ensure the successful implementation and continuation of a comprehensive, integrated approach to teacher evaluation, the superintendent needs to affirm and reaffirm his or her commitment to the program. In the early stages of the reform, the superintendent demonstrates this commitment by showing symbolic support for the effort to improve the quality of teaching in the district. As the reform is implemented, the superintendent manifests commitment either by serving as the program's "fixer" or by appointing a trusted assistant to carry out this important function. The primary responsibility of the "fixer" is to monitor the implementation process and to solve the problems that inevitably arise as it unfolds.

Once the reform is successfully implemented the superintendent must continue to show his or her interest in the evaluation function and instructional improvement. Unless the superintendent persists in nurturing the importance of accountability and improvement, these goals will be slighted for more urgent problems and issues.

Although the cost of putting this comprehensive approach to teacher evaluation into practice is probably high, the costs of retaining incompetent teachers may be even higher. A district that ignores its incompetent teachers may undermine the political support of parents and taxpayers, lower the morale of its competent teachers, and, most importantly, diminish the educational opportunities of its students. Conversely, a district that deals forthrightly with its unsatisfactory teachers can expect to increase public confidence in its institutional effectiveness; to preserve, if not raise, the morale of its teaching staff; and to provide all of its students with a meaningful and adequate education.

Appendix

District Evaluation Practices Inventory (DEPI)

	TRUE OF OUR DISTRICT			
	YES	NO	?	COMMENTS
1. "Excellence in Teaching" is a high priority in the district. (Pg. 9)	☐	☐	☐	
a. Superintendent provides symbolic leadership. (Pg. 9)	☐	☐	☐	
b. Superintendent and board establish priorities relating to the supervision and evaluation of teachers prior to negotiations. (Pg. 11)	☐	☐	☐	
c. Superintendent and board allocate funds that are targeted for evaluating, assisting, and dismissing teachers. (Pg. 1 1)	☐	☐	☐	
d. Superintendent examines the district's approach to evaluation and dismissal in a systematic manner. (Pg. 11)	☐	☐	☐	
e. Superintendent promotes cooperation with other districts in matters relating to the evaluation and dismissal of teachers. (Pg. 12)	☐	☐	☐	
2. Has adopted and published reasonable criteria for judging the competence of teachers (Pg. 13)	☐	☐	☐	
a. Criteria are legally defensible. (Pg. 13)	☐	☐	☐	
b. Criteria are professionally defensible. (Pg. 15)	☐	☐	☐	

© 1990. This inventory should be used in conjunction with *Managing the Incompetent Teacher*, 2nd ed., by E. Bridges and B. Groves. ERIC Clearinghouse on Educational Management, University of Oregon, Eugene.

	TRUE OF OUR DISTRICT			
	YES	NO	?	COMMENTS
c. Criteria are scientifically defensible. (Pg. 16)	☐	☐	☐	
d. Supervisors are able to suggest specific indicators of unsatisfactory performance for each criterion. (Pg. 16)	☐	☐	☐	
e. Supervisors are able to prescribe remediation for deficiencies in relation to each criterion. (Pg. 18)	☐	☐	☐	
3. Uses sound procedures for determining whether teachers meet each criterion. (Pg. 19)	☐	☐	☐	
a. Uses supervisory ratings. (Pg. 19)	☐	☐	☐	
b. Uses student ratings. (Pg. 22)	☐	☐	☐	
c. Uses student performance on tests. (Pg. 23)	☐	☐	☐	
d. Uses peer evaluations. (Pg. 26)	☐	☐	☐	
e. Uses self-evaluations. (Pg. 27)	☐	☐	☐	
f. Uses parent evaluations. (Pg. 29)	☐	☐	☐	
g. Uses student and parent complaints. (Pg. 30)	☐	☐	☐	
h. Uses a combination of above. (Pg. 32)	☐	☐	☐	
4. Provides assistance and a reasonable time to improve. (Pg. 33)				
a. Identifies causes of poor performance; looks for: (Pg. 34)	☐	☐	☐	
1. Managerial, organizational shortcomings. (Pg. 34)	☐	☐	☐	
2. Employee shortcomings. (Pg. 34)	☐	☐	☐	
3. Outside influences. (Pg. 34)	☐	☐	☐	
b. Provides various types of remediation such as: (Pg. 35)	☐	☐	☐	
1. Goal setting. (Pg. 35)	☐	☐	☐	

Appendix 75

	TRUE OF OUR DISTRICT			
	YES	NO	?	COMMENTS
2. Instructional input. (Pg. 35)	☐	☐	☐	
3. Modeling. (Pg. 35)	☐	☐	☐	
4. Practice. (Pg. 36)	☐	☐	☐	
5. Feedback. (Pg. 36)	☐	☐	☐	
6. Coaching. (Pg. 36)	☐	☐	☐	
7. Reinforcement. (Pg. 37)	☐	☐	☐	
8. Therapy. (Pg. 37)	☐	☐	☐	
9. Counseling. (Pg. 37)	☐	☐	☐	
10. Environmental change. (Pg. 37)	☐	☐	☐	
c. Provides period to improve. (Pg. 38)	☐	☐	☐	
1. Length of time reasonable. (Pg. 38)	☐	☐	☐	
2. Timing of assessments appropriate. (Pg. 39)	☐	☐	☐	
3. Proper treatment of back-sliders. (Pg. 39)	☐	☐	☐	
5. Supervisors have requisite competencies and district has taken steps to ensure supervisors have these competencies. (Pg. 41)	☐	☐	☐	
a. Supervisors are able. . .	☐	☐	☐	
1. to make systematic classroom observations. (Pg. 41)	☐	☐	☐	
2. to provide unbiased ratings. (Pg. 43)	☐	☐	☐	
3. to diagnose the cause(s) of a teacher's poor performance. (Pg. 45)	☐	☐	☐	
4. to prescribe appropriate remediation. (Pg. 46)	☐	☐	☐	
5. to conduct conferences with teachers. (Pg. 47)	☐	☐	☐	
6. to document matters related to (a.1)-(a.5). (Pg. 48)	☐	☐	☐	
b. Supervisors know the legal basis for evaluating and dismissing teachers. (Pg. 50)	☐	☐	☐	
c. District promotes these competencies in supervisors through. . .	☐	☐	☐	
1. Selection. (Pg. 51)	☐	☐	☐	
2. In-service education. (Pg. 51)	☐	☐	☐	
3. Printed materials. (Pg. 51)	☐	☐	☐	

	TRUE OF OUR DISTRICT			
	YES	NO	?	COMMENTS
6. Provides the necessary resources. (Pg. 53)	☐	☐	☐	
a. Time. (Pg. 53)	☐	☐	☐	
b. Authority. (Pg. 54)	☐	☐	☐	
c. Access to remedial assistance. (Pg. 55)	☐	☐	☐	
d. Access to legal counsel. (Pg. 56)	☐	☐	☐	
e. Backing and emotional support (Pg. 57)	☐	☐	☐	
7. Holds supervisors accountable. (Pg. 58)	☐	☐	☐	
a. Has policies to discourage inflated ratings. (Pg. 58)	☐	☐	☐	
b. Counters tendencies to procrastinate and rationalize. (Pg. 59)	☐	☐	☐	
c. Discourages the practice of "passing the turkey." (Pg. 60)	☐	☐	☐	
d. Evaluates principals on their instructional leadership. (Pg. 61)	☐	☐	☐	
8. Provides a fair hearing prior to dismissal. (Pg. 63)	☐	☐	☐	
a. Hearing procedures are legally defensible. (Pg. 63)	☐	☐	☐	
b. Supervisors are prepared to handle the discovery, direct examination, and cross-examination phases of the hearing. (Pg. 64)	☐	☐	☐	

Managing the Incompetent Teacher

Bibliography

Many of the items in this bibliography are indexed in ERIC's monthly catalog *Resources in Education* (*RIE*). Reports in *RIE* are indicated by an "ED" number. Journal articles that are indexed in ERIC's companion catalog, *Current Index to Journals in Education*, are indicated by an "EJ" number.

Most items with an ED number are available from the ERIC Document Reproduction Service (EDRS), 3900 Wheeler Ave., Alexandria, VA 22304-6409.

To order from EDRS, specify the ED number, type of reproduction desired—microfiche (MF) or paper copy (PC), and number of copies. Add postage to the cost of all orders and include check or money order payable to EDRS. For credit card orders, call 1-800-227-3742.

Acheson, K., and Gall, M. *Techniques in the Clinical Supervision of Teachers.* New York: Longman, 1987. ED 278 159.

Aleamoni, L. M. "Student Ratings of Instruction." In *Handbook of Teacher Evaluation,* edited by J. Millman. 110-45. Beverly Hills, California: SAGE Publications, Inc., 1981.

Anderson, H. "A Study of Certain Criteria of Teaching Effectiveness." *Journal of Experimental Education* 23 (September 1954): 41-71.

Beckham, J. "Legally Sound Criteria, Processes and Procedures for the Evaluation of School Professional Employees." *Journal of Law and Education* 14, 4 (October 1985): 529-51. EJ 331 362.

Benzley, J.; Kauchak, D.; and Peterson, K. "Peer Evaluation: An Interview Study of Teachers Evaluating Teachers." Paper presented at the annual meeting of the American Educational Research Association, Chicago, 1985. 23 pages. ED 260 099.

Block, J. *Mastery Learning in Classroom Instruction.* New York: Macmillan, 1975.

Bloom, B. "The Two-Sigma Problem: The Search for Methods of Group Instruction as Effective as One to One Tutoring." *Educational Researcher* 13, 6 (1984): 4-16. EJ 303 699.

Bridges, E. "Evaluation for Tenure and Dismissal." In *Handbook of Teacher Evaluation,* edited by J. Millman and L. Darling-Hammond. Beverly Hills, California: Sage, 1989.

———. "Faculty Evaluation—A Critique and a Proposal." *Administrator's Notebook* 22, 6 (1974): 1-4.

———. *The Incompetent Teacher.* Philadelphia, Pennsylvania: Falmer Press, 1990.

[77]

_____. *The Management of Incompetence.* Stanford, California: Institute for Research on Educational Finance and Governance, 1983. Technical Report.

_____. "Managing the Incompetent Teacher—What Can Principals Do?" *NASSP Bulletin* 69, 478 (February 1985): 57-65. EJ 311 740.

Bridges, E. M., and Gumport, P. *The Dismissal of Tenured Teachers for Incompetence.* Stanford, California: Institute for Research on Educational Finance and Governance, 1984. Technical Report.

Brieschke, P. "The Administrative Role in Teacher Competency," *The Urban Review* 18, 4 (1986): 237-51. EJ 356 379.

Brookover, W. "Person-Person Interaction Between Teachers and Pupils and Teaching Effectiveness." *Journal of Educational Research* 34, 4 (December 1940): 272-87.

Bryan, R. C. *Reactions to Teachers by Students, Parents, and Administrators.* United States Office of Education, Cooperative Research Project, No. 668. Kalamazoo, Michigan: Western Michigan University, 1963. ED 002 785.

Buellesfield, H. "Causes of Failure among Teachers." *Educational Administration and Supervision* 1 (September 1915): 439-45.

Bush, A. J., and Kennedy, J. J. "An Empirical Investigation of Teacher Clarity." *Journal of Teacher Education* 28, 2 (March - April 1977): 53-58.

Capie, W. *Teacher Performance Assessment Instruments and Staffs of the Teacher Assessment Project, Performance-based Certification Unit and Regional Assessment Centers.* Atlanta: Georgia Department of Education, Division of Staff Development 1983.

Carey, W. C. *Documenting Teacher Dismissal.* Salem, Oregon: Options Press, 1981.

Centra, J. A. *Determining Faculty Effectiveness.* San Francisco: Jossey-Bass, 1979. ED 183 127.

Citron, C. "An Overview of Legal Issues in Teacher Quality." *Journal of Law and Education* 14, 3 (July 1985): 277-307. EJ 327 901.

Claxton, W. "Remediation: The Evolving Fairness in Teacher Dismissal." *Journal of Law and Education* 15, 2 (Spring 1986): 181-93. EJ 337 547.

Cohen, E. *Designing Group Work.* New York: Teachers College Press, 1986.

Cohen, P. "Effectiveness of Student-Rating Feedback for Improving College Instruction." *Research in Higher Education* 13, 4 (1980): 321-41.

_____. "Student Ratings of Instruction and Student Achievement." *Review of Educational Research* 51, 3 (Fall 1981): 281-309.

Corwin, R., and Wagenaar, T. "Boundary Interaction Between Service Organizations and Their Problems: A Study of Teacher-Parent Relationships." *Social Forces* 55 (1976): 471-92.

Cramer, J. "How Would Your Faucets Work If Plumbers Were Shielded by Tenure Laws?" *The American School Board Journal* (October 1976): 22-24.

Dolgin, A. "Two Types of Due Process: The Role of Supervision in Teacher Dismissal Cases." *NASSP Bulletin* 65, 442 (February 1981): 17-21.

Downey, G. W. "How to Get Rid of Your Bad Teachers and Help Your Good Ones Get Better." *American School Board Journal* 165, 6 (June 1978): 23-26.

Eash, M.; Rasher, S.; and Waxman, H. "Evaluating Teacher Behavior from Student Perceptions." *Studies in Educational Evaluation* 6 (1980): 293-95.

Educational Research Service. *Negotiating the Teacher Evaluation Issue.* Arlington, Virginia: ERS, Inc., 1979. ED 170 960.

Elam, S. M., ed. *A Decade of Gallup Polls of Attitudes Toward Education 1969-1978.* Bloomington, Indiana: Phi Delta Kappa, 1978. 382 pages. For results of polls conducted since 1979, see the September issues of the *Phi Delta Kappan.* ED 166 834.

Emmer, E. T., and others. *Organizing and Managing the Junior High Classroom.* Austin, Texas: The Research and Development Center for Teacher Education, R&D Report No. 6151, 1982. ED 223 564.

Epstein, J. "A Question of Merit: Principals' and Parents' Evaluations of Teachers." *Educational Researcher* 14, 7 (August/September 1985): 3-10. EJ 323 028.

Evans, D. "Reflections of a Principal on the Procedures for the Dismissal of a Permanent Teacher." Mimeographed.

Evertson, C. M., and Emmer, E. T. "Effective Management at the Beginning of the School Year in Junior High Classes." *Journal of Educational Psychology* 74, 4 (1982): 485-98. EJ 267 792.

Evertson, C.M., and others. *Organizing and Managing the Elementary School Classroom.* Austin, Texas: The Research and Development Center for Teacher Education, 1981. ED 223 570.

Finlayson, H. J. "Incompetence and Teacher Dismissal." *Phi Delta Kappan* 61, 1 (September 1979): 69.

Fisher, C. W., and others. "Teaching Behaviors, Academic Learning Time, and Student Achievement: An Overview." In *Time to Learn,* edited by C. Denham and A. Lieberman. Washington, D. C.: National Institute of Education, 1980. 251 pages. ED 192 454.

Fox, R.; Peck, R.; Blattstein, A.; and Blattstein, D. "Student Evaluation of Teacher as a Measure of Teacher Behavior and Teacher Impact on Students." *Journal of Educational Research* 77, 1 (September/October 1983): 16-21.

Freiberg, H. "Teacher Self-Evaluation and Principal Supervision." *NASSP Bulletin* 71, 498 (April 1987): 85-92. EJ 353 844.

Frels, K., and Cooper, T. T. *A Documentation System for Teacher Improvement or Termination.* Topeka, Kansas: National Organization on Legal Problems of Education, 1982. 24 pages. ED 228 725.

___. *A Documentation System for Teacher Improvement or Termination.* Practical Concise Guide for Legal Consideration in Teacher Evaluation. Revised. Topeka, Kansas: National Organization on Legal Problems of Education, 1986. ED 269 890.

French-Lazovik, G. "Peer Review." In *Handbook of Teacher Evaluation,* edited by J. Millman. 73-89. Beverly Hills, California: SAGE Publications, Inc., 1981.

Gage, N. L. "Improving Instruction: Ideas Superintendents Can Give Principals to Help Teachers." *School Administrator* 40 (May 1983): 23-26.

___. *The Scientific Basis of the Art of Teaching.* New York: Teachers College Press, 1978.

Gage, N. L.; Runkel, P. J.; and Chatterjee, B. B. *Equilibrium Theory and Behavior Change: An Experiment in Feedback from Pupils to Teachers.* Report No. 6 in Studies in the Generality and Behavioral Correlates of Social Perception.

Bureau of Educational Research, College of Education, University of Illinois, 1960.

Gold, C.; Dennis, R. E.; and Graham, J. "Reinstatement after Termination: Public School Teachers." *Industrial and Labor Relations Review* 31 (April 1978): 310-21.

Gotham, R. "Personality and Teaching Efficiency." *Journal of Experimental Education* 14, 2 (December 1945): 157-65.

Gross, J. *Teachers on Trial.* Ithaca, New York: ILR Press, 1988.

Groves, B. "An Organizational Approach to Managing the Incompetent Teacher." Unpublished Ed.D. dissertation, Stanford University, 1985.

Guthrie, H. D., and Willower, D. J. "The Ceremonial Congratulation: An Analysis of Principal Observation Reports of Classroom Teaching." *High School Journal* 56, 6 (March 1973): 284-90.

Haertel, E. "The Valid Use of Student Performance Measures for Teacher Evaluation." *Educational Evaluation and Policy Analysis* 8, 1 (Spring 1986): 45-60. EJ 350 184.

Hallinger, P. J. *Assessing the Instructional Management Behavior of Principals.* Unpublished Ed.D. dissertation, School of Education, Stanford University, 1983.

Harper, W. P., and Gammon, R. T. "Defining Inadequate Performance under the North Carolina Tenured Teacher Fair Dismissal Act." *Campbell Law Review* 3, 77-102.

Hoge, R. D., and Luce, S. "Predicting Academic Achievement from Classroom Behavior." *Review of Educational Research* 49 (1979): 479-96.

Hook, C. M., and Rosenshine, B. V. "Accuracy of Teacher Reports of Their Classroom Behavior." *Review of Educational Research* 49,1 (Winter 1979): 1-12.

Hoover, N., and Carroll, R. "Self-Assessment of Classroom Instruction: An Effective Approach to Inservice Education." *Teaching and Teacher Education* 3, 3 (1987): 179-91. EJ 362 953.

Hunter, M. Publications and audiovisual materials available through TIP Publications, El Segundo, California.

Janis, I. L., and Mann, L. *Decision Making.* New York: The Free Press, 1977.

Jayne, C. "A Study of the Relationship Between Teaching Procedures and Educational Outcomes." *Journal of Experimental Education* 14, 2 (December 1945): 101-34.

Jones, D. L. *Arbitration and Industrial Discipline.* Ann Arbor, Michigan: Bureau of Industrial Relations, The University of Michigan, 1961.

Jones, R. D. "The Prediction of Teaching Efficiency from Objective Measures." *Journal of Experimental Education* 15 (1946): 85-99.

Joyce, B., and Showers, B. "Improving Inservice Training: The Messages of Research." *Educational Leadership* 37, 5 (February 1980): 379-85.

____. "Transfer of Training: The Contribution of 'Coaching'." *Journal of Education* 163, 2 (Spring 1981): 163-72.

Joyce, B.; Showers B.; and Rolheiser-Bennett, C. "Staff Development and Student Learning: A Synthesis of Research on Models of Teaching." *Educational Leadership* 45, 2 (October 1987): 11-23.

Karweit, N. L. *Time on Task: A Research Review.* Baltimore, Maryland: Center for

Social Organization of Schools, Johns Hopkins University, January 1983. Report No. 332. ED 228 236.

Kauchak, D.; Peterson, D.; and Driscoll, A. "An Interview Study of Teachers' Attitudes Toward Teacher Evaluation Practices." *Journal of Research and Development in Education* 19, 1 (Fall 1985): 32-37. EJ 328 824.

Kaufman, H. G. *Professionals in Search of Work.* New York: John Wiley and Sons, 1982.

Kennedy, M. "Things That Can Go Awry When Tests Are Used to Manage Instruction." *Evaluation Comment* 6, 3 (1983): 8-9.

Kerman, S. "Teacher Expectations and Student Achievement." *Phi Delta Kappan* 60 (June 1979): 716-18.

Kerr, D. H. "Teaching Competence and Teacher Education in the United States." In *Handbook of Teaching and Policy*, edited by L. S. Shulman and G. Sykes: 126-49. New York: Longman, 1983.

Kowalski, J. *Evaluating Teacher Performance.* Arlington, Virginia: Educational Research Service, 1978.

LaDuke, C. "The Measurement of Teaching Ability." *Journal of Experimental Education* 14, 1 (September 1945): 75-100.

Larson, D. H. "Advice for the Principal: Dealing with Unsatisfactory Teacher Performance." *NASSP Bulletin* 65, 442 (February 1981): 10-11.

Latham, G. P., and Wexley, K. N. *Increasing Productivity Through Performance Appraisal.* Reading, Massachusetts: Addison-Wesley Publishing Company, 1981. (Pages 48-64).

Lebeis, C. "Teacher Tenure Legislation." 37 *Michigan Law Review*, 430 (1939).

Lefton, R., and others. *Effective Motivation Through Performance Appraisal.* Cambridge, Massachusetts: Ballinger Publishing Company, 1980. (Pages 200-229).

Lins, L. J. "The Prediction of Teaching Efficiency." *Journal of Experimental Education* 15 (1946): 2-60.

Littler, S. "Why Teachers Fail." *Home and School Education* 33 (March 1914): 255-56.

Lortie, D. *The Schoolteacher: A Sociological Study.* Chicago: University of Chicago Press, 1975.

Luehe, F. W., and Ehrgott, R. H. *Target Teaching.* Visalia, California: Key Publications, 1981.

Mackenzie, R. A. *The Time Trap.* New York: McGraw-Hill Book Company, 1972.

Madsen, I. N. "The Prediction of Teaching Success." *Educational Administration and Supervision* 13 (January 1927): 39-47.

Mager, R. *Analyzing Performance Problems.* Belmont, California: Fearon Publishers, 1970.

Maier, N. R. F. *The Appraisal Interview.* La Jolla, California: University Associates, Inc., 1976.

Malinowski, A. A. "An Empirical Analysis of Discharge Cases and the Work History of Employees Reinstated by Labor Arbitrators." *Arbitration Journal* 36, 1 (March 1981): 31-46.

McCall, W., and Krause, G. "Measurement of Teacher Merit." *Journal of Educational Research* 53, 2 (October 1959): 73-75.

McCarthey, S., and Peterson, K. "Peer Review of Materials in Public School Teacher Evaluation," *Journal of Personnel Evaluation in Education* 1, 3 (1988): 259-68.

McDaniel, S. H., and McDaniel, T. R., "How to Weed out Incompetent Teachers without Getting Hauled into Court." *National Elementary Principal* 59, 3 (March 1980): 31-36.

McDermott, T. J., and Newhams, T. H. "Discharge - Reinstatement: What Happens Thereafter." *Industrial and Labor Relations Review* 24, 4 (July 1971): 526-40.

McDonnell, L., and Pascal, A. *Organized Teachers in American Schools.* Santa Monica, California: Rand Corporation, 1979. 122 pages. ED 175 123.

McLaughlin, M. "The Lake Washington (Washington) School District No. 414 Teacher Evaluation System." In *Case Studies for Teacher Evaluation: A Study of Effective Practices*, edited by A. Wise, L. Darling-Hammond, M. McLaughlin, and H. Bernstein. 37-87. Santa Monica, California: The Rand Corporation, 1984. N-2133-NIE. ED 251 952.

McLaughlin, M., and Pfeifer, S. *Teacher Evaluation: Improvement, Accountability, and Effective Learning.* New York: Teachers College Press, 1988. ED 291 727.

McNeil, J. D. "Politics of Teacher Evaluation." In *Handbook of Teacher Evaluation*, edited by J. Millman. 272-91. Beverly Hills, California: SAGE Publications, Inc., 1981.

Medley, D., and Coker, H. "The Accuracy of Principals' Judgments of Teacher Performance." *Journal of Educational Research* 80, 4 (March/April 1987): 242-47. EJ 354 931.

Medley, D.; Coker, H.; and Soar, R. *Measurement-Based Evaluation of Teacher Performance.* New York: Longman, 1984.

Medley, D., and Mitzel, H. "Some Behavioral Correlates of Teacher Effectiveness." *The Journal of Educational Psychology* 50, 6 (December 1959): 239-46.

Miller, L. M. *Behavior Management.* New York: John Wiley and Sons, Inc., 1978.

Millman, J. "Student Achievement as a Measure of Teacher Competence." In *Handbook of Teacher Evaluation*, edited by J. Millman. 146-66. Beverly Hills, California: SAGE Publications, Inc., 1981.

Miner, J., and Brewer, J. "The Management of Ineffective Performance." In *Handbook of Industrial and Organizational Psychology*, edited by M. Dunnette. 995-1030. Chicago: Rand-McNally, 1976.

Mitchell, T.; Green, S.; and Wood, R. "An Attributional Model of Leadership and the Poor Performing Subordinate." In *Research in Organizational Behavior*, edited by L. L. Cummings and B. M. Staw. 197-234. New York: JAI Press Inc., 1981.

Moore, K. "Supervisor's Manual on Certificated Evaluations and Dismissal." Chino Unified School District, California, 1980. (Mimeographed).

Munnelly, R. J. "Dealing with Teacher Incompetence: Supervision and Evaluation in a Due Process Framework." *Contemporary Education* 50, 4 (Summer 1979): 221-25.

National Education Association, "Evaluation of Teaching Competence." *NEA Research Bulletin* 47, 3 (December 1969): 2-9.

Natriello, G., and Dornbusch, S. M. "Pitfalls in the Evaluation of Teachers by

Principals." *Administrator's Notebook* 29, 6 (1980-81). EJ 261 536.

Neill, S. B., and Custis. *Staff Dismissal: Problems and Solutions*. Arlington, Virginia: American Association of School Administrators, 1978. 80 pages. ED 172 417.

Nolte, M. C. "How to Tell Which Teachers to Keep and Which to Lay Off." *American School Board Journal* (September 1975): 28-30.

O'Reilly, C. A., and Weitz, B. A. "Managing Marginal Employees: The Use of Warnings and Dismissals." *Administrative Science Quarterly* (1980): 467-84.

Palker, P. "How to Deal with Incompetent Teachers." *Teacher* 97, 4 (January 1980): 44-45.

Peck, C. *Compensating Salaried Employees During Inflation: General vs. Merit Increases*. New York: The Conference Board, Report No. 796, 1981.

Peterson, K. D. "The Principal's Tasks." *Administrator's Notebook* 26 (1977-78): 1-4.

Pfeifer, R.S. "Variations on a Theme: An Analysis of Peer Involvement in Teacher Evaluation." Paper presented at the annual meeting of the American Educational Research Association, Washington, D.C., 1987. 43 pages. ED 285 882.

Phay, R. E. *Legal Issues in Public School Administrative Hearings*. Topeka, Kansas: National Organization on Legal Problems in Education, 1982. ED 217 524.

Popham, W. J. "Alternative Teacher Assessment Strategies." Working paper for a meeting of the Multi-State Consortium on Performance-Based Teacher Evaluation, New Orleans, Louisiana, February 1973.

Remers, H. H. "Reliability and 'Halo' Effect of High School and College Students' Judgments of Their Teachers." *Journal of Applied Psychology* 18 (October 1939): 619-30.

Rippey, R. *The Evaluation of Teaching in Medical Schools*. New York: Springer Publishing Company, 1981. ED 197 636.

Roper, S., and Hoffman, D. *Collegial Support for Professional Development: The Stanford Collegial Evaluation Program*. Eugene: Oregon School Study Council, University of Oregon, March 1986. OSSC Bulletin Series. 36 pages. ED 275 067.

Rosenberg, A. *Setting the Tone*. Oakland, California: Oakland Public Schools, 1987.

Rosenberger, D. S., and Plimpton, R. A. "Teacher Incompetence and the Courts." *Journal of Law and Education* 4, 3 (July 1975): 468-86.

Rosenshine, B. "Enthusiastic Teaching: A Research Review." *School Review* (August 1970): 499-514.

_____. "The Stability of Teacher Effects upon Student Achievement." In *The Appraisal of Teaching*, edited by G. Borich. 341-50. Reading, Massachetts: Addison-Wesley Publishing Company, 1977.

_____. *Teaching Behaviors and Student Achievement*. London: National Foundation for Educational Research in England and Wales, 1971.

Rowe, M. "Wait-Time and Rewards as Instructional Variables, Their Influence on Language, Logic, and Fate Control." *Journal of Research in Science Teaching* 11 (1974): 81-94.

Scriven, M. "Duty-Based Teacher Evaluation." *Journal of Personnel Evaluation in Education* 1, 4 (July 1988): 319-34.

Seely, J. G. *Personal Communication.* December 12, 1983.

Simon, D. L. "Personal Reasons for the Dismissal of Teachers in Smaller Schools." *Journal of Educational Research* 29, 8 (April 1936): 585-88.

Slavin, R. *Cooperative Learning.* New York: Longman, Inc., 1983.

Sproull, L. "Managing Educational Programs." *Human Organization* 40 (1981): 113-22.

Stalnecker, J. M., and Remers, H. H. "Can Students Discriminate Traits Associated with Success in Teaching?" *Journal of Applied Psychology* 12 (December 1929): 605ff.

Steinmetz, L. L. *Managing the Marginal and Unsatisfactory Performer.* Reading, Massachusetts: Addison-Wesley Publishing Company, 1969.

Stelzer, L., and Banthin, J. *Teachers Have Rights, Too.* Boulder, Colorado: ERIC Clearinghouse for Social Studies/Social Science Education, 1980. 176 pages. ED 199 144.

Stone, C. "A Meta-Analysis of Advance Organizer Studies." *Journal of Experimental Education* 51, 4 (1983): 194-99.

Stringfield, S., and Hartman, A. "Irregularities in Testing: Ethical, Psychometric, and Political Issues." Paper presented at the annual meeting of the American Educational Research Association, April, 1985, Chicago, Illinois.

Thurston, P. "Dismissal of Tenured Teachers in Illinois: Evolution of a Viable System." (forthcoming)

_____ . "Tenured Teacher Dismissal in Illinois, 1975-79." *Illinois Bar Journal* 69, 7 (March 1981): 422-31.

Tigges, J. "What Constitutes 'Incompetency' or 'Inefficiency' as a Ground for Dismissal or Demotion of Public School Teachers." 4 ALR 3d 1090.

Tolleson, R. *Certificated Non-Management Personnel Assessment Manual.* Carmichael, California: San Juan Unified School District, 1989.

Tuckman, B. W., and Oliver, W. F. "Effectiveness of Feedback to Teachers as a Function of Source." *Journal of Educational Psychology* 59, 4 (1968): 297-301.

Wade, R. "What Makes a Difference in Inservice Teacher Education? A Meta-Analysis of Research." *Educational Leadership* 42, 4 (December 1984/January 1985): 48-54. EJ 311 595.

Waxman, H. C., and Walberg, H. J. "The Relation of Teaching and Learning: A Review of Reviews of Process-Product Research." *Contemporary Education Review* 1, 2 (Summer 1982): 103-20.

Wise, A.; Darling-Hammond, L.; McLaughlin, M.; and Bernstein, H. *Teacher Evaluation.* Santa Monica, California: Rand Corporation, 1984. ED 246 559.

Other Publications

At-Risk Families and Schools: Becoming Partners

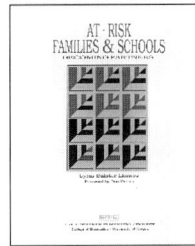

Lynn Balster Liontos • Foreword by Don Davies • 1992 • xii + 156 pages • perfect (sew/wrap) bind • ISBN 0-86552-113-1 • $12.95.

This book shows educators how to reach out to families who are poor, belong to racial/ethnic minorities, or speak a language other than English. The book contains many examples of effective programs along with Liontos's own recommendations for school boards, administrators, and teachers.

In the foreword, Don Davies calls Liontos's book "a welcome gift to all of us," in that it pulls together "various strands of theory, research, and demonstration" in order to give educators a basis for thinking about at-risk families and the roles they play in schools.

The Collaborative School: A Work Environment for Effective Instruction

Stuart C. Smith and James J. Scott • Foreword by Roland S. Barth • 1990 • xii+77 pages • perfect (sew/ wrap) bind • ISBN 0-86552-092-5 • $9.00. (Copublished with NASSP)

What are *collaborative schools*? In contrast to many schools where the adults work in isolation from one another, teachers and administrators in collaborative schools work as a team. Through such practices as mutual help, exchange of ideas, joint planning, and participation in decisions, the faculty and administrators improve their own skills and the effectiveness of their schools.

This book outlines the educational benefits of collaboration, describes a variety of collaborative practices already in use in schools, and suggests ideas for introducing those practices in other schools that wish to become more collaborative.

School Leadership: Handbook for Excellence

Edited by Stuart C. Smith and Philip K. Piele • Second Edition • 1989 • xvi + 392 pages • perfect (sew/wrap) bind • ISBN 0-86552-096-8 • $17.95.

This handbook suggests the knowledge, structure, and skills necessary for a leader to inspire all members of the school community to work together toward the goal of an excellent education for every student.

Rather than summarizing research findings as an end in itself, each chapter includes one or more sections that spell out implications, recommendations, or guidelines for putting knowledge into practice. The book is also, as Edwin M. Bridges says in the foreword, "highly readable."

Part 1. The Person
• Portrait of a Leader •Leadership Styles
• Training and Selecting School Leaders
• Two Special Cases: Women and Blacks

Part 2. The Structure
• School-Based Management • Team Management • Participative Decision-Making
• School Climate

Part 3. The Skills
• Leading the Instructional Program
• Leading the Instructional Staff • Communicating • Building Coalitions • Leading Meetings • Managing Time and Stress
• Managing Conflict

Graying Teachers: A Report on State Pension Systems and School District Early Retirement Incentives

Frank V. Auriemma, Bruce S. Cooper, Stuart C. Smith • Foreword by Richard D. Miller • 1992 •

x + 92 pages • 8 ¹/2 x 11 • perfect (sew/wrap) bind • ISBN 0-86552-118-2 • $12.50.

This report presents a complete state-by-state overview of the retirement programs available to America's teachers. In addition, case studies of early retirement incentive plans in six districts provide some useful information about how these plans work: amounts spent and saved, numbers of teachers eligible to retire early versus those who take the option, and the costs of replacing the teachers who retired.

Keith Geiger of NEA: "A timely, comprehensive, and invaluable resource."

Richard Miller of AASA: "Case studies in this book give useful data and methods for evaluating the effectiveness of various teacher retirement incentive plans."

Problem-Based Learning for Administrators

Edwin M. Bridges, with the assistance of Philip Hallinger • 1992 • xii + 164 pages • perfect (sew/wrap) bind • ISBN 0-86552-117-4 • $10.95.

PBL is a training strategy in which students, working in groups, take responsibility for solving professional problems. The instructor creates a hypothetical situation for the students (called a *project*) and then takes a back seat as an observer and an advisor while the students work out a solution.

Professor Bridges has spent the last five years developing, field testing, and refining PBL for use in educational management classes, and this book is the record of what he has learned. Using student essays, detailed descriptions of actual projects, data from PBL in the medical field, and his own observations, Bridges illustrates how PBL teaches leadership, management, and communication skills to administrative students.

Albert Shanker of the AFT says, "Problem-Based Learning . . . should bring a revolution to the professional development of principals."

VALUE SEARCHES

Value Searches—economical, user friendly collections of ERIC resumés—are available on the following topics:
- School Restructuring
- School Choice, Vouchers, and Open Enrollment
- Parent Involvement in the Educational Process
- Instructional Leadership
- Leadership of Effective Schools
- Collegiality, Participative Decision-Making and the Collaborative School

The searches have been purged of irrelevant citations and laser printed for easy readability. The introduction to each *Value Search* lists the index terms used for the search and the time period covered—in most cases, the last five years. Instructions for using the citations, which include bibliographic information and abstracts, and for ordering copies of the complete documents and journal articles are included.

Every Value Search is updated several times each year. The price is $7.50 each (buy 4 titles and get 1 free).

Working Together: The Collaborative Style of Bargaining

Stuart C. Smith, Diana Ball, and Demetri Liontos • Foreword by Charles Taylor Kerchner • 1990 • xii + 75 pages • saddle bind • ISBN 0-86552-103-4 • $7.25.

In some school districts, teacher unions and district officials are exchanging an adversarial style of labor relations for a more cooperative process that emphasizes problem-solving, mutual respect, and team involvement in the education process. This book's descriptions of collaborative bargaining practices being tried by various school districts, along with practical guidelines and pitfalls to avoid, make the volume a good starting-point for educators interested in adopting a more collaborative process.

Full payment or purchase order must accompany all orders. A handling charge ($3.00 domestic, $4.00 international) is added to all billed orders. Make checks payable to **University of Oregon/ERIC**. Address orders to ERIC/CEM, 1787 Agate Street, Eugene, OR 97403. (800) 438-8841. FAX: (503) 346-2334. Expect 6-8 weeks for delivery. (To expedite delivery, you may specify UPS for an extra charge.)